IDEOLOGY

David Hawkes

LONDON AND NEW YORK

First published 1996
by Routledge
11 New Fetter Lane, London EC4P 4EE

Simultaneously published in the USA and Canada
by Routledge
29 West 35th Street, New York, NY 10001

© 1996 David Hawkes

Typeset in Adobe Garamond and Scala Sans by
Keystroke, Jacaranda Lodge, Wolverhampton

Text design by Mark Bedford

Printed and bound in Great Britain by
Clays Ltd, St. Ives PLC

British Library Cataloguing in Publication Data
A catalogue record for this book is available from the British Library

Library of Congress Cataloguing in Publication Data
Hawkes, David, 1964–
    Ideology / David Hawkes.
        p.   cm. — (The new critical idiom)
    Includes bibliographical references.
        ISBN 0–415–09808–4 (hardcover). — ISBN 0–415–09809–2 (pbk).
    1. Criticism.   2. Literature and society.   I. Title.   II. Series.
PN81.H298   1996
    801′.95—dc20   95–39942
                                                                CIP

ISBN 0–415–09808–4 (hbk)
ISBN 0–415–09809–2 (pbk)

In memory of my grandmother, Betty Roberts

CONTENTS

SERIES EDITOR'S PREFACE

The New Critical Idiom is a series of introductory books which seeks to extend the lexicon of literary terms, in order to address the radical changes which have taken place in the study of literature during the last decades of the twentieth century. The aim is to provide clear, well-illustrated accounts of the full range of terminology currently in use, and to evolve histories of its changing usage.

The current state of the discipline of literary studies is one where there is considerable debate concerning basic questions of terminology. This involves, among other things, the boundaries which distinguish the literary from the non-literary; the position of literature within the larger sphere of culture; the relationship between literatures of different cultures; and questions concerning the relation of literary to other cultural forms within the context of interdisciplinary studies.

It is clear that the field of literary criticism and theory is a dynamic and heterogeneous one. The present need is for individual volumes on terms which combine clarity of exposition with an adventurousness of perspective and a breadth of application. Each volume will contain as part of its apparatus some indication of the direction in which the definition of particular terms is likely to move, as well as expanding the disciplinary boundaries within which some of these terms have been traditionally contained. This will involve some re-situation of terms within the larger field of cultural representation, and will introduce examples from the area of film and the modern media in addition to examples from a variety of literary texts.

PREFACE

Why another book on ideology, especially at a time when political and philosophical developments have cast significant doubt on the use and value of this concept? Because this book argues for a particular understanding of ideology as a description of the very conditions which have brought the notion of ideology into question. It suggests that the most convincing accounts of ideology have portrayed it as a false consciousness resulting from the belief in the autonomy and determining power of representation. It claims that this belief is characteristic of and analogous to, though not necessarily determined by, market capitalism, and it traces a consistent historical pattern in the various critiques to which this mental tendency has been subjected since the beginning of the capitalist era. It does not attempt to catalogue the infinity of definitions which has been offered for the term 'ideology', but instead argues for the historical primacy, philosophical validity, and continued postmodern relevance of one particular definition.

Terry Eagleton was the first to direct my interest to the subject of ideology, and his own work in this area has been a consistent source of inspiration. John Drakakis and Talia Rodgers have been unfailingly kind and supportive editors. Barbara Traister and Dympna Callaghan read drafts of the manuscript and weeded out many infelicities, and Ted Byfield helped me out in the final stages. I have benefited greatly from discussions with Bill Brewer, Mark Bevir, Helen Steward and Eve Moros. Maureen Perry was generous with her time and her advice, and I shall always be grateful to her.

INTRODUCTION:

Ideology and the Postmodern

You know the people I mean. Girls who subliminally model themselves on kid-show presenters, full of faulty melody and joy, Melody and Joy. Men whose manners show newscaster interference, soap stains, film smears. Or the cretinized, those who talk on buses and streets as if TV were real, who call up networks with strange questions, stranger demands. . . . If you lose your rug, you can get a false one. If you lose your laugh, you can get a false one. If you lose your mind, you can get a false one.

(Martin Amis, *Money*)[1]

A false mind? Is such a thing possible? We are accustomed, in everyday conversation, to refer to people's 'false' smiles, their 'false' laughs, any number of 'false' attitudes they choose to present to the world. We call such people 'insincere', meaning that their outward appearance, their image, does not accurately reflect their internal, 'real' or 'true' feelings. But what if the interior self, the mind, were itself artificial? What if the core of a person's identity, his 'personality', was nothing more than a conglomeration of images and attitudes assimilated from the external environment?

In that case, it would make no sense to criticize someone because his image failed to correspond to his 'true' personality. The very concept of an independent personality which could be separated from someone's material actions would be brought into serious question. What would be the consequences for the human condition of such a development?

Martin Amis's blackly comic novel *Money* (1984) describes the experience of someone with an entirely artificial, or 'false', personality. John Self, the book's narrator and anti-hero, is unable to distinguish between the 'real' world, and the world as it is represented in the media. This results in a pronounced ethical deterioration; the only values he can appreciate are material wealth and sensual gratification. Self has no self other than a nexus of physical impulses and desires, which can be sated through the medium of money. He represents, in fact, the archetypal consumer. Hedonistic, materialist, vacuous, he consumes commodities, alcohol and women indifferently and insatiably. Furthermore, through his job directing advertisements for television, Self spends his professional life trying to manipulate others into becoming like him. It is as if money had entered into Self's soul, expelling any pristine personality, and re-shaping him according to its own requirements. It is in this sense that, as he himself is aware, his mind is becoming 'false'. Most disturbingly, Amis's work suggests that the future belongs to people like Self. In fact, Self represents nothing less than the personification of the self in its postmodern form. What do we understand by this term?[2]

The postmodern era begins with the shift of Western society away from industrial production, and towards consumption and exchange-based economies. This process started in the early twentieth century, rapidly gathered pace after the Second World War, and further intensified in the credit-fuelled, deregulated markets of the 1980s. The history of capitalism since 1945 is dominated by the dramatic self-assertion of the media of representation. Money, for example, is originally a symbol used to represent material objects, so that they can be exchanged. But in a market economy, this representation becomes an end in itself, shouldering aside the substantive things which it symbolizes and dominating the global economy of the postmodern world. It moves further and further away from any grounding in reality, becoming progressively more abstract as it takes the form of precious metals, banknotes, figures on computer screens, credit, interest and investor 'confidence'. At the same time, money becomes an active or subjective power, so that the minutest fluctuations in the relationships between the various forms of money have profound effects on the material lives of human beings throughout the world. We can thus say that the postmodern economy is characterized by the autonomy of representation.

This economic development has taken place alongside a corresponding rise to cultural prominence of the technological media of representation. From cinema, radio and television to video, compact discs and the internet, the twentieth century has witnessed an unprecedented explosion in the number and kinds of images to which people are exposed every day. Since these media are usually run with the aim of making a profit by selling commodities or advertising space, the result has been to bombard the population with incessant injunctions to purchase goods and services. The lack of hard cash is no longer an obstacle to consumption; people receive countless letters and telephone calls offering easy credit, along with suggestions about what to spend it on. Political debate in the Western democracies no longer revolves around substantive issues. Instead, the candidates for office market themselves like any other products, and their most valued advisers are 'spin doctors' and media consultants. We live in the era of the Image.

Postmodern philosophy is also characterized by the autonomy of representation. Semiotics and deconstruction challenge the nineteenth-century realist belief that linguistic signs simply point towards real things in a transparent and uncomplicated fashion.

Rather, it is suggested, what we perceive as the 'real' world is created for us, or constructed, by the signifying systems we use to represent it. This has led many postmodernist thinkers to question whether the concept of ideology is still relevant. The word 'ideology' usually designates a way of thinking which is systematically mistaken, a false consciousness. If, however, we believe in the power of representation to construct reality, the distinction between truth and falsehood becomes hard to maintain. There may be 'truth-effects', produced by various signifying systems, or discourses, but there can be no external standard of judgement according to which we could evaluate their claims. This is why postmodern philosophy is often described as a kind of relativism – it asserts that claims to truth are only valid with reference to a particular discourse, and that there is therefore no privileged perspective of absolute truth from which one might accuse others of error.

What is more, postmodernism disputes the very existence of an independent consciousness, or autonomous subject. If there is no experience without representation, then the media of representation must be prior even to our experience of our own selves. In fact, it is argued, the self is produced by the interaction of signifying systems which allocate it a particular identity without any independent volition on its part. This is one of the most radical and innovative claims made by postmodernism. It rejects as 'idealist' any suggestion that the human mind contains an element – a 'soul' or a 'self' – which can be distinguished from the way the subject represents itself in material form. As the philosopher Richard Rorty puts it:

> The crucial move in this reinterpretation is to think of the moral self, the embodiment of rationality, not as . . . somebody who can distinguish her *self* from her talents and interests and views about the good, but as a network of beliefs, desires, and emotions with nothing behind it – no substrate behind the attributes.[3]

The self does not exist in the pure realm of ideas, but only as it is represented in tangible, material form. Another way of putting this is to say that the subject has become objectified. Western philosophy traditionally divides existence into two categories – a human 'subject' which experiences the world and forms ideas about it, and an 'object' which is the mass of external, material things which exists outside the subject. Postmodernism refuses this binary opposition of subject and object. It declares that the first term of this dichotomy is produced and defined by the latter, reducing the subject to an illusory unity artificially imposed on an intersection of objective practices. Once again, this challenges the pertinence of the term 'ideology'. The notion of false consciousness becomes redundant if the concept of an independent consciousness is itself illusory. All consciousness then becomes artificial, and therefore 'false' only in the sense that an artificial limb is false.

Postmodernism also departs from traditional philosophy in its opposition to the 'totality'. The best way to understand this concept is to consider the binary opposition discussed above, between the subject (the consciousness which perceives the world), and the object (the external phenomena which are perceived). It has long been recognized that such oppositions are mutually definitive. It would be impossible to conceive of a perceiving subject unless we also had the concept of something which is external to the subject, and which could therefore be perceived by it. Similarly, the concept of an object of perception would be meaningless without the notion of an active subject which could do the perceiving. Thus, although the terms 'subject' and 'object' are indeed opposites, they are also constitutive of each other – they make each other possible. They interpenetrate, forming an overarching unity, or totality, which is more than the sum of its parts.

Postmodernism agrees that concepts are defined by what they are not, by their 'other'. The identity of the subject is only established in relation to the object, and vice versa. Post-modernism refuses, however, to draw from this the conclusion that the two poles of this opposition form a unified totality, insisting instead on the irreducible difference between the individual elements. It is able to do this because of its belief in the autonomy of representation. In order to relate to each other, subject and object must be represented in language; this is the medium in which the subject establishes its identity, and through which it experiences the object. However, postmodernism argues that the medium of representation is prior to, and constitutive of, the elements between which it supposedly mediates.[4] It follows that the categories of 'subject' and 'object' are only linguistic functions. Since, according to the postmodern view, linguistic signs achieve meaning only by virtue of their difference from each other, the terms of the subject/object dichotomy must therefore remain distinct from each other, and cannot be subsumed within an overriding totality.

This assault on the notion of totality has further implications for the postmodern condition.[5] Earlier ways of thinking assumed the existence of a transcendental subject. From the interpenetration of subject and object, and their subsumption beneath a unified totality, it was held to follow that all phenomena were finally interconnected within an ultimate, originary unity. To take only the most obvious example, Christianity expresses the unity of such oppositions as subject and object, universal and particular, ideal and material, in the doctrine of the Incarnation, which sub-sumes them under the overarching totality of 'God'. The concepts of the 'soul' and of its descendant the autonomous subject, fulfil a similar unifying function with regard to the human condition. By elevating a core of subjectivity above the flux of material events, they make it possible to believe that the history of the human race and the course of an individual life are being guided by a consciousness which transcends the concrete circumstances of history. This is often referred to as the narrative or teleological conception of history, since it assumes that history progresses towards an ultimate end or purpose. Postmodernism rejects this idea as 'totalizing', arguing instead that history is a discontinuous succession of events with no transcendent purpose or meaning. Since totality and teleology have historically offered convincing standards by which ideas can be judged as correct or erroneous, postmodernity's scepticism towards these concepts further erodes the validity of the concept 'ideology'.

These, then, are the three major ideas which are under attack in the postmodern era: (1) the referential model of representation, (2) the autonomous subject, (3) the totality, whether this takes the form of history as a whole, or of the whole of society. These concepts have been criticized in the past, but never with the kind of success which currently attends postmodernism both within and beyond the academy. The cumulative effect is to suggest that human thought really is entering a new era, and that there is no place in this era for the notion of ideology as false consciousness.

But what has brought these new ideas into being? One possible answer is that human beings are becoming cleverer, that our thought develops through time, revealing past errors and new truths as it progresses. According to its own tenets, however, postmodernism would have to reject this postulate for, as we have seen, it refuses to countenance any such teleological view of history. It seems, then, that we must look for an explanation beyond the self-contained history of thought, and try to connect postmodernism to the wider social, economic and political climate in which it flourishes.

As I have suggested above, the last fifty years have witnessed a dramatic expansion in the power and influence of the capitalist market economy. Institutions dedicated to the interests of capital, such as the IMF and the World Bank, have become far more important than any national government. Intervention by these governments to impede the unrestricted free-play of market forces is no longer tolerated. In the West, the concerted effort to transform people into consumers has greatly intensified. Entire industries – advertising, marketing, packaging – are explicitly dedicated to serving capital by manipulating people into purchasing particular products. Very recently, the market has been able to expand into areas of the globe from which it had previously been forcibly excluded. Surely any observer would agree that the second half of the twentieth century has been dominated by the rise to absolute pre-eminence of capital and the free-market economy?

Not so. Although postmodernism presents itself as a radical or 'oppositional' mode of thought, its opposition to 'totalizing' explanations blinds many of its adherents to this ostensibly indisputable fact. Here is Andrew Ross, chastising old-fashioned leftism for its failure to get with the postmodernist programme:

> the left's view of Capital itself as a supremely rational and monolithic, domination-producing system has tended to remain in place. . . . Capital, or rather, our imaginary of Capital, still belongs for the most part to a demonology of the Other. This is a demonology that inhibits understanding and action as much as it artificially keeps alive older forms of *ressentiment* that have little or no purchase on a postmodern consumer society.[6]

Postmodernists hover between asserting (in denial of all the evidence) that capital is not the determining factor in the postmodern world, and suggesting that even if it is, the pleasures of consumerism are so delightful as to remove any regrettable associations still clinging to the market economy. Why is this? Could it be that there is a convergence of interest between late capitalism and postmodern theory? Let us return to the three major tenets of postmodernism which we identified earlier, and see whether any of them might serve the purposes of a capitalist market economy.

First, we found that postmodernism celebrates the autonomy

of representation. We have already seen how money, a form of representation, grows progressively more autonomous with the development of capitalism. As the economy moves away from the production of material, substantive things, and instead becomes dominated by commodity exchange, which takes place through the medium of financial representation, we might expect that philosophy will place more determining power upon signifying systems, even to the extent of claiming that these form the only knowable reality. This would certainly seem to bolster the market economy's assumption that money is not merely a system of signs pointing to substantive things, but that it has an inherent value.

Second, postmodernism attacks the autonomous subject, on the grounds that the 'self' is in fact nothing more than the intersection of various representational discourses. Does market capitalism use representation to mould and manipulate people's personalities? Do the industries of advertising and marketing determine people's patterns of behaviour, self-image or opinions? Our society is now so deeply committed to the consumer mentality that it is difficult to see anything pernicious in the thousands of corporate messages to which we are all forcibly exposed every day. This plethora of images can seem entirely harmless; it is even sometimes presented as liberating the natural libidinous energy of desire. Paul Bové speaks for many when he claims that

> The shift of capital from production to consumption along with the development of advertising and other aspects of the 'production of signs' has released desire from some of the more familiar and repressive forms of bourgeois reproduction.[7]

It is always difficult to evaluate a phenomenon which is so ubiquitous. As postmodernism suggests, it is hard to find a privileged perspective from which to judge the various discourses which construct us. A judicious temporal or cultural distance, however, can sometimes bring the issue into sharper focus. Consider the following advertisements from the 1920s:

LISTERINE (1923)

Edna's case was really a pathetic one. Like every woman, her primary ambition was to marry. Most of the girls of her set were married – or about to be. Yet not one possessed more grace or charm or loveliness than she.

And as her birthdays crept gradually toward that tragic thirty-mark, marriage seemed farther from her life than ever.

She was often a bridesmaid but never a bride.

That's the insidious thing about halitosis (unpleasant breath). You, yourself, rarely know when you have it. And even your closest friends won't tell you.

THE BOOK OF ETIQUETTE (1925)

For him she is wearing her new frock. For him she is trying to look her prettiest. If only she can impress him – make him like her – just a little.

Across the table he smiles at her, proud of her prettiness, glad to notice that others admire. And she smiles back, a bit timidly, a bit self-consciously.

What wonderful poise he has! What complete self-possession! If only *she* could be so thoroughly at ease. . . . She wasn't sure of herself, she didn't *know*. And she discovered, as we all do, that there is only one way to have complete poise and ease of manner, and that is to know definitely what to do and say on every occasion.

LUCKY STRIKE CIGARETTES (1929)

Instead of eating between meals . . . instead of fattening sweets . . . beautiful women keep youthful slenderness these days by smoking Luckies. The smartest and loveliest women of the modern stage take this means of keeping slender . . . when others nibble fattening sweets, they light a Lucky!

That's why there's real health in Lucky Strike. That's why folks say: 'Its good to smoke Luckies.'

... They know that Luckies steady their nerves and do not harm their physical condition. They know that Lucky Strike is the favorite cigarette of many prominent athletes, who must keep in good shape ...[8]

It may well be that we have no access to any privileged position from which to judge the above. But there is surely a prima facie case for assuming that these extremely successful advertisements deliberately inculcate certain modes of thought and behaviour, that they do so by creating or consolidating artificial insecurities and prejudices, that they do this for their own profit, and that the net result is harmful and destructive both to the individual and to society as a whole. It seems probable that, while today's advertisements are considerably more subtle than those cited above, they are nevertheless engaged in a similarly self-interested manipulation of human desires and aspirations. In other words, it is reasonable to suppose that, in the words of one recent commentator, capitalist corporations systematically propagate 'the concept of the human being as an insatiable, desiring machine or as an animal governed by an infinity of desires'.[9] Once again, this bears an uncanny resemblance to the picture of the subject painted by postmodernist philosophy.

Third, postmodernism criticizes the tendency to refer individual phenomena to their context within a totality. Its emphasis on difference insists that we view things as discrete, heterogeneous objects, rather than as parts of a social whole. It also dictates that historical events must be considered as isolated incidents in a discontinuous process, rather than as chapters in a larger story, or steps on the road to some ultimate *telos*. However, it is only the concept of the totality which enables us to think of identity as relational. Totalizing modes of thought suggest that isolated phenomena can only be truly understood if placed in relation to the whole of society and seen in the overall context of human history. This context can provide a standard by which we can

particular practices and events. If, for example, we place
alist mentality in the context of human history, we will
soon discover that it is a new, unique, anomalous approach to life
which, in the words of Max Weber, 'would both in ancient times
and in the Middle Ages have been proscribed as the lowest form
of avarice and as an attitude entirely lacking in self-respect'.[10] So it
helps to perpetuate the *status quo* if people believe that things
and events are best studied in isolation, away from the totalities of
society or history.

Above all, postmodernism challenges the concept of ideology
as false consciousness. The autonomy of representation removes
our access to any absolute criterion of truth; the destruction of
the autonomous subject throws doubt upon the existence of an
independent consciousness; the attacks on totality and teleology
remove the contexts against which the discrete appearances of
today's society might be found wanting. As we have seen, however,
postmodernism does all this in the interests of market capitalism.
There is, then, a sense in which ideology's validity as an interpretative category is demonstrated in the very act of attacking it.
One of the most venerable conceptions of ideology is as a system
of thought which propagates systematic falsehood in the selfish
interest of the powerful and malign forces dominating a particular
historical era. By that definition, postmodernism is nothing more
than the ideology of consumer capitalism.

1

ORIGINS

The earth was without form and void, and darkness was upon the face of the deep; and the Spirit of God was moving over the waters

(Genesis 1:1)

THE SOURCES OF FALSE CONSCIOUSNESS

We should note at the outset that the suspicion with which postmodern culture views the concept of false consciousness is unprecedented. In the past, civilizations have generally developed sophisticated criteria to demonstrate the errors of their victims or rivals. The Greeks declared foreigners to be uncivilized, primitive 'barbarians' who lacked the gift of rational thought; the early Christians portrayed pagans as sinful, worldly 'idolaters', addicted to the things of this world and the pleasures of the flesh. It is beyond the scope of this book to analyse such ancient discourses in detail. For our purposes, the relevant task is to describe the theories of false consciousness which typify the modern world. In order to do this, however, we will first need to mention the essential Greek and biblical understandings of the relation between spirit and matter.

The belief that the world, or our experience of the world, is created out of a union between matter and spirit is as old as Western thought itself. The history of philosophy consists of a protracted attempt to think through the relationship between these elements. This means introducing a third term – representation – which will mediate between the two poles of the dichotomy. In the Introduction, we saw how the postmodern era is marked by the autonomy of representation. As their name implies, the postmodern ideas we discussed in the Introduction emerged as a reaction against the characteristic assumptions of the 'modern' age. The modern period begins with the sixteenth century and stretches until the middle of the twentieth. It is the era of production-based capitalism, as opposed to the exchange-oriented postmodern economy. In sharp contrast to postmodernism, the philosophy of the modern period is profoundly absorbed in the identification and refutation of false consciousness. During the 'early modern' period of the sixteenth and seventeenth centuries, western Europe began its long process of mutation from an agricultural, feudal society into one organized around a capitalist, money-based economy. People began to think about themselves and the world around them in new ways, ways which are characteristic of the modern world. This meant that they had to engage in a struggle against the old, entrenched assumptions which they were displacing. The modern notion of ideology was first developed as a weapon in that battle, and the rediscovery of ancient Greek philosophy, combined with the translation of the Bible into the vernacular, provided the thinkers of the Renaissance period with ammunition against the entrenched ideas of the Church and the state.

All modern theories of false consciousness claim that it is produced by an imbalance in the tripartite relationship between the subject (which is the realm of ideas), the object (the world of substantial, material things), and the media of representation which negotiate between these two poles. These three elements make up a totality. When one set of ideas, or 'discourse', intends to label another as false, it always declares that its opponent has misunderstood the relations between the three parts of this totality. This tactic can be traced to the very beginning of Western philosophy. In Plato's *Republic*, for example, ideas are held to be more authentic than the material world. If we take the objective world for reality, we commit an error which is simultaneously an ethical transgression. Plato likens the way human beings perceive the material world to the vision of prisoners chained by the neck in a cave. A fire burns behind them, and a wall runs between the prisoners and the fire. Plato then describes

> men carrying along that wall, so that they overtop it, all kinds of artifacts, statues of men, reproductions of other animals in stone or wood fashioned in all sorts of ways, and . . . some of the carriers are talking while others are silent.[1]

The prisoners would only be able to see the shadows thrown on the wall by these artifacts, and would thus naturally take these shadows to be real things and assume that the voices of the men emanated from the shadows. Any prisoner who escaped into the sunlight and returned to tell his fellows about the real world would be treated as a malicious lunatic by the denizens of the cave. Plato means to indicate that the visible world is made up of mere shadows of ideal forms, which are inaccessible to normal human perception. Not only is this perception flawed, he suggests, but it is in the nature of this flaw to disguise itself, so that it appears self-evident to human beings that the visible world is the only real one. We should also note that the shadows are cast by man-made objects: carved figures, which are carried by human beings. Deliberate deception is thus involved in constructing this pattern of illusion, and this theme will recur frequently in the history of ideology.

After Plato, Hellenic thought generally takes for granted the superiority of the ideal over the material. This means that the mutually definitive binary opposition between ideas and matter has become a hierarchy, in which the former pole is privileged over the latter. We can see some of the consequences of this in Aristotle's *Politics*. In that work, all forms of power are justified by analogy with the mind/body hierarchy:

> It is then in an animal . . . that one can first discern both the sort of rule characteristic of a master and political rule. For the soul rules the body with the rule characteristic of a master, while intellect rules appetite with political and kingly rule; and this makes it evident that it is according to nature and advantageous for the body to be ruled by the soul, and the passionate part [of the soul] by intellect and the part having reason, while it is harmful to both if the relation is equal or reversed.[2]

From the presupposition that the mind's subjective ideas are naturally superior to the objective material body, Aristotle proceeds to deduce the necessary dominance of masters over slaves, of Greeks over barbarians, and of men over women. A bias in the relation of the ideal to the material gives credence to the claim that certain human beings are fit only to be ruled by others, as well as to the assertion that certain forms of consciousness are systematically false.

Aristotle goes on to identify further errors in thought, which he traces to distortions of the relations between ideas, things and representations. He claims, for instance, that every piece of property can be regarded in two ways:

> Every possession has a double use. Both of these uses belong to it as such, but not in the same way, the one being proper and the other not proper to the thing. In the case of footwear, for example, one can wear it or one can exchange it.
>
> (1257al, 7–10)

If the use of the shoe is simply to be worn, it can be regarded as a material object. If on the other hand the shoe is to be exchanged for another object, or sold, an ideal form must be grafted on to the material thing. The shoe is then not simply a shoe, it must be conceived as equivalent to the object for which it is to be exchanged. We must impose an idea on the object which does not naturally belong to its material properties. For this to be possible on any large scale, a common denominator is necessary. We need a sphere of representation which can mediate between the shoe in itself and our idea of the shoe. According to Aristotle, this medium is money. As long as it retains its proper place as a go-between for the ideal and the material, Aristotle looks benignly upon money. When it becomes an end in itself, however – when money is used merely to generate more money – he considers that a fundamental logical and ethical error has been made:

> expertise in exchange is justly blamed since it is not according to nature but involves taking from others, usury is most reasonably hated because one's possessions derive from money itself and not from that for which it was supplied. For it came into being for the sake of exchange, but interest actually creates more of it. . . . So of all sorts of business this is the most contrary to nature.
>
> (1258bl, 41–8)

Once again, this error results from an imbalance in the proper relations between ideas, matter and representation. When the medium of representation becomes autonomous, when it is exalted above the elements between which it supposedly mediates, an unnatural and perverse view of the world is the result.

The Hebraic tradition, which along with Hellenic thought is the primal influence on Western philosophy, also ascribes false consciousness to a misconstruction of the relations between the elements of the totality. In the Hebrew Bible, the Israelites are distinguished from the gentiles by the prohibition on material representations of their deity. Due to the attraction which sensual things hold for fallen humanity, such representations will inevitably become fetishes; that is, people will forget that they are merely representations, and idolize them, venerating them as though they were incarnations of the divine. Yahweh makes this clear when, in the first two commandments, He makes the abandonment of images a precondition of monotheism:

> **Exodus 20:3.** Thou shalt have no other gods before me. **4.** Thou shalt not make unto thee any graven image, or any likeness of any thing that is in heaven above, or that is in the earth beneath, or that is in the water under the earth. **5.** Thou shalt not bow down thyself to them, nor serve them: for I the Lord thy God am a jealous God, visiting the iniquity of the fathers upon the children unto the third and fourth generation of them that hate me.

The ferocity of the aniconic commandment is necessary because, due to our faulty understanding of the relation between signs and things, we will inevitably mistake an image of God for God Himself. Representations of the deity are thus incompatible with Judaic monotheism, which asserts that the source of all meaning is an absolute *logos* which is necessarily incorporeal. It is therefore fundamentally erroneous to worship an image. But it is also immoral to do so, for two reasons. First of all, an image is a material object, and thus ethically inferior to the ideal dimension of the divine. Second, an image is the product of human labour – it has been 'graven', or manufactured. In worshipping an icon, then, we are really worshipping the objectified manifestation of our own labour. This aspect of idolatry was particularly stressed under the Babylonian captivity. The book of Isaiah contains lengthy descriptions of the various kinds of labour which go into manufacturing the Babylonian icons, and the fact that they have been produced by human labour is cited as the clearest possible proof of the absurdity of worshipping images:

Isaiah 41:18. To whom then will ye liken God? Or what likeness will ye compare unto him? **19.** The workman melteth a graven image, and the goldsmith spreadeth it over with gold, and casteth silver chains. **20.** He that is so impoverished that he hath no oblation chooseth a tree that will not rot; he seeketh unto him a cunning workman to prepare a graven image, that shall not be moved.

Isaiah 46:5. To whom will ye liken me, and make me equal, and compare me, that we may be like? **6.** They lavish gold out of the bag, and weigh silver in the balance, and hire a goldsmith; and he maketh it a god: they fall down, yea, they worship.

What is being criticized here is the attempt to establish an equivalence between the ideal and the material through the use of representation. Such an enterprise succeeds only in fetishizing the products of human labour, bestowing upon them a superstitious power and an illegitimate influence over human life. In the New Testament, the Hebraic proscription of idols blends with Hellenic idealism, issuing in a generalized mistrust of all earthly perception, which will only be corrected by posthumous heavenly revelation. Thus Paul, writing to the Corinthians:

I Corinthians 13:12. For now we see through a glass, darkly; but then face to face: now I know in part; but then shall I know even as I am known.

The Platonic–Christian tradition thus assumes that it is impossible for human beings to see things in their true nature. It establishes an 'idealist' hierarchy, in which earthly, material knowledge is necessarily imperfect. But Greek thought also offers a more sanguine view of the possibility of overcoming false consciousness. In the *Magna Moralia*, Aristotle considers the relationship between 'nature' and 'custom'. The distinction rests on the difference between innate and acquired characteristics, and Aristotle suggests that the former are the more durable:

> For nothing that is by nature becomes other by custom. For instance, a stone, and heavy things in general, naturally go downwards. If anyone, then, throws them up repeatedly, and tries to accustom them to go up, all the same they would never go up, but always down.[3]

Clearly, to attempt to alter the nature of natural objects is a task of Sisyphean futility. In the sphere of human nature, however, the nature/custom dichotomy becomes less absolute. Human beings habitually conduct themselves in ways which, while they may remain constant, are evidently not 'natural' in the same sense as the law of gravity. In book II of the *Magna Moralia*, Aristotle restates the primacy of nature over custom, but this time with a rather different emphasis:

> For what comes by nature is harder to cure than what comes by custom (for the reason why custom is held to be so strong is that it turns things into nature).

(1203b, 31)

It seems that we are to distinguish between two kinds of nature. On the one hand the term refers to intrinsic, immutable qualities, such as weight in the stone. On the other, there are customary modes of behaviour which can become so habitual that they come to appear natural. This 'second nature' is different from the first in that it can be changed, and manipulated. It therefore has a powerful potential as an agent of social control. In fact, in the *Nicomachean Ethics*, Aristotle presents the cultivation of this 'second nature' as a fundamental element of statecraft:

> This is confirmed by what happens in states; for legislators make the citizens good by forming habits in them, and this is the wish of every legislator; and those who do not effect it miss their mark, and it is in this that a good constitution differs from a bad one.[4]

This operation on the part of political leaders may strike modern readers as underhand, even sinister. If it does, this testifies to our assumptions that social development and adaptation are, broadly speaking, good things; that people ought to evaluate situations and determine courses of action by means of rational analysis; and that it is foolish to continue doing things in a certain way merely because that is how they have been done in the past. To Aristotle, on the contrary, habit and custom are the foundations of morality and civilization, and any legislator who neglects to cultivate these qualities in his subjects is failing in his duty. Despite this, we can find in the Aristotelian concept of a 'second nature' the basis of a theory of false consciousness which allows for the possibility that such faulty thinking, being the product of human invention, might be overcome.

THE DAWN OF MODERNITY

When early modern thinkers felt the need to criticize particular ideas as false, they returned to these ancient sources, whose teachings became proverbial commonplaces. For example, the notion of 'idolatry' – the worship of images – was frequently used to describe a generalized false consciousness, whose secular manifestations were understood as similar in kind to its religious applications. Thus the seventeenth-century poet George Herbert castigates pagan idolatry as a confusion of means and ends, but notes that his own society operates under a similar delusion:

> Ah, what a thing is man devoid of grace!
>   Adoring garlic with an humble face,
> Begging his food of that which he may eat,
>   Starving the while he worshippeth his meat . . .
>
> None will believe this now, though money be
>   In us the same transplanted foolery.[5]

Herbert thus finds the venerable biblical statement that 'covetousness' is idolatry confirmed by the practices of his contemporaries. In similar fashion, Fulke Greville's 'Treatise of Monarchy' (c.1610) justifies political authority in straightforwardly Aristotelian terms. This long poem opens with a reflection on the harmonious relation between rulers and subjects which supposedly characterized the mythical 'golden age'. This mutual respect and understanding, Greville claims, was possible only 'Before this art of power allay'd the trueth' (l.23).[6] There follows a detailed account of this 'allaying', which is seen to accompany the 'declination' of monarchy to tyranny. Its ultimate effect is to deprive the subjects of any volition, either in deciding how they will be governed or in choosing what beliefs to follow. People become, as Greville puts it, mere 'blankes where pow'r doth write her lust' (l.326). 'Power', a force which is personified throughout the poem, acquires the ability to form and mould its subjects according to its needs. Greville expresses this relationship by means of a simile: 'That as the heads *Ideas* rule the heart/Soe pow'r might print her will in every part' (ll.377–8). The seminal manifestation of power can thus be found in the haughty dominance of the mind over the body; and the source of hierarchy is again traced to an imbalance between the subjective and the objective spheres.

However, the people of the early modern era were attempting to come to terms with dramatic changes in the organization of social life. A simple transposition of Greek and biblical notions seemed inadequate to explain the unprecedented experiences of modernity. One way of differentiating modern ways of thinking about false consciousness from earlier ones is to chart people's changing attitudes towards precedent, or 'custom'.[7] Around the beginning of the sixteenth century, the idea began to be formulated that, far from guaranteeing ethical action as Aristotle had argued, a blind adherence to custom represented a superstitious and unwarranted reverence for past forms of social behaviour. This notion at first emerged only haltingly, out of the need to explain and legitimate local civil and ecclesiastical innovations. The chaos inflicted on Italy in 1494 by the invasion of Charles VIII of France, for instance, produced extremely sudden and dramatic political changes, which called forth new theories of secular power. Following the flight of Florence's hereditary ruler, Piero de' Medici, the affairs of the city-state were briefly directed by a fanatically puritanical monk named Girolamo Savonarola. In accordance with scholastic tradition, Savonarola justified his seizure of power in Aristotelian terms:

> Habit, indeed, is second nature, and as the rock's nature is to fall and it cannot alter this and cannot be raised except by force, so habit too becomes nature, and it is very difficult if not impossible to change men, especially whole peoples, even if their habits are bad, for their habits spring out of their character.
>
> Now the Florentine people, having established a civil form of government long ago, has made such a habit of this form that, besides suiting the nature and requirements of the people better than any other, it has become habitual and fixed in their minds. It would be difficult, if not impossible to separate them from this form of government.[8]

In fact, as Savonarola and his audience were well aware, Florence had not had 'a civil form of government' – that is to say, it had not been a republic – for sixty years. But because the only available vocabulary for legitimating power involved an appeal to custom, Savonarola was forced into the paradoxical position of invoking tradition to justify revolutionary innovation.

In practice, Savonarola's four-year rule was characterized by rather bizarre and obsessive attempts to destroy and obliterate all manifestations of the nefarious 'second nature'. A particular target of the monk's ire was the practice of wearing make-up, or 'face painting', and cosmetics were frequently incinerated, along with other sinful, worldly artifacts, in public 'bonfires of the vanities'.

The principal objection to wigs, powder and face-paint was that they made it possible to fabricate a new identity, and thus appeared to be an arrogation of the divine prerogative of creation. This 'second nature' was understood to be idolatrous, because it replaced the works of God with the work of human beings. In his anti-cosmetic diatribes, Savonarola was able to formulate an account of 'second nature' as a distortion and perversion of the God-given 'first' nature. Perhaps this explains the priority he gave to what today may seem a peripheral issue: it provided an opportunity for theoretical advances which was unavailable in overtly political discourse.

By thus attempting to reform long-established, customary behaviour while lacking a theoretical justification for political innovation, Savonarola soon made himself unpopular, and he was overthrown and executed in 1498. A younger Florentine, Niccolò Machiavelli, drew from this the conclusion that an innovative ruler must disseminate a systematic illusion among his subjects if he is to retain power. Savonarola, declares Machiavelli in *The Prince*, was an 'unarmed prophet',

> who was ruined in his new orders when the multitude began not to believe in him, and he had not the means of keeping firm those who had believed, or to make unbelievers believe.[9]

The Prince considers the question of how a reforming ruler can legitimate his reign. Machiavelli claims that the question does not arise in the case of hereditary princes, or with regard to a ruler who does not seek to introduce social or cultural change. In such circumstances, an appeal to custom is sufficient to forestall rebellion. To keep people obedient:

> it is enough, not to transgress the arrangements of their ancestors . . . it is reasonable that . . . [the prince] will be well liked by his subjects, and the memories and causes of innovations are lost in the ancientness of the continuation of his

> Dominion . . . in maintaining their old condition, and there not
> being differences in customs, men will live quietly.
>
> (238–9)

The question raised by the recent history of Florence, however,
was how a government which desires to abolish old customs
and introduce new ones might justify itself in the eyes of its
subjects. Obviously, such a government cannot honestly invoke
established custom. And yet Machiavelli did not have access to any
other vocabulary in which power could be legitimated. The only
possible solution for an innovative government, he concludes, is to
deceive the people. As he puts it in the *Discourses*:

> He who desires or wants to reform the State of a City, and
> wishes that it may be accepted and capable of maintaining
> itself to everyone's satisfaction, it is necessary for him at
> least to retain the shadow of ancient forms, so that it does not
> appear to the people that the institutions have been changed,
> even though in fact the new institutions should be entirely
> different from the past ones: for the general mass of men are
> satisfied with appearances, as if it exists, and many times are
> moved by the things which appear to be rather than by the
> things that are.
>
> (330)

When skilfully deployed, it seems, mere representations can
pass themselves off as reality. Machiavelli has thus described two
distinct forms of false consciousness. There is, first of all, the
tendency of the people to make a fetish out of their past modes of
behaviour, or custom. Machiavelli perceives a natural human
urge to continue doing things as they have, apparently, always been
done. This essentially involves mistaking second nature for the first
nature. It is as if the actions people have performed in the past
acquire an animate power in the present and work to frustrate
progress and disguise society's real interests, so that, as Machiavelli

puts it later, 'the People desire their own ruin' (363). But this self-deception on the part of the people necessitates a second deception which is deliberately instigated by their ruler, who must falsely represent any innovations as if they were continuations of established practice. It thus appears that ideology (to use the anachronism) can arise spontaneously out of quotidian social life, and that it can also be inculcated through a conscious manipulation of 'appearances' by the powers that be. This attribution of a deceptive element to the civil power was so shocking to Renaissance sensibilities that Machiavelli's name soon became a byword for cunning and intrigue in general. Thus, in Marlowe's *The Jew of Malta* (1590), the prologue uses the Florentine's name as a noun, which tells the audience all they need to know about the villanous protagonist, Barabas: 'you shall find him still/ In all his projects a sound Machevill/ And that's his character' (ll.7–9).

Despite his unsavoury reputation over the century following his death, Machiavelli's work both described and facilitated a radical change in political thought. The ideas that the people's attachment to custom can constitute a brake on good government, and that it can be desirable for the government to deceive the people amounted to a transformation in the conventional conception of civil power. One good reason for locating the decisive historical break between the 'medieval' and the 'modern' worlds in the early sixteenth century is the fact that an analogous development in religious thought took place simultaneously with Machiavelli's breakthrough in the secular realm. *The Prince* was written in 1512, and in 1517 (tradition has it) Martin Luther nailed his ninety-five theses to the church door at Wittenberg.

The intellectual revelation which initiated the Reformation came when Luther recognized the causal link between the two great problems which beset him: his inability to free himself from guilt through any amount of monastic discipline, and the presence in Wittenberg of the indulgence-seller Johann Tetzel.

As an Augustinian monk, Luther had distinguished himself by his insatiable zeal for penance. His exasperated confessor would frequently dismiss him with the injunction not to return until he had some real sins to expiate. And yet Luther found that he was unable to convince himself of God's forgiveness, or to assure himself of his salvation, through the performance of penitential labour, or 'works'.

The idea that absolution from sin can be achieved by carrying out certain ecclesiastically mandated tasks was central to Catholic belief, and penance was a holy sacrament. It was thus in the Pope's power to impose penitential fasts, pilgrimages, banishments and so on to enable sinners to expiate their transgressions. As well as imposing them, the Pope could also excuse offenders from these penalties. This was often done by calculating a cash equivalent of the penance imposed, and substituting this fine for the performance of the penitential works. This remission became known as an 'indulgence'. This practice was widely deemed acceptable, as long as it was made clear that the money bought remission only from the temporal punishment, and that to buy an indulgence was to participate in a purely legal transaction with the worldly aspect of papal power. Over the two centuries preceding Luther, however, the talismanic potency attached to indulgences increased to the degree that they were believed to be capable of purchasing for the owner a reduction of the time he or she would have to spend in purgatory. Although the papacy disclaimed such views, unscrupulous indulgence-peddlers found it paid to encourage them. The rhyme against which Luther complains in the ninety-five theses – 'when you hear the money's ring, the soul from purgatory springs'[10] – accurately summarizes the popular misconception fostered by indulgence-hawkers.

An indulgence, then, was a certificate denoting a specific amount of human activity. The indulgence system represented these penitential works in the form of a currency. Salesmen like Tetzel attributed to these certificates the power to ameliorate the condition of the soul in the afterlife. One way of putting this would be to say that indulgences represented fetishized labour. They were representations of human actions, which were ascribed supernatural, magical power in the popular imagination. Their role was essentially financial. Just as money establishes a medium of representation which enables us to conceive of an equivalence between human labour and various objects, so indulgences provided a common denominator which made it possible to imagine an equivalence between penitential tasks and divine grace. The Church was supposed to control a kind of capital treasury of the surplus good works of the saints, from which it could dole out specific amounts in exchange for the cash of the indulgence-purchasers. Luther's initial protest was supposedly against a local 'abuse' of this system perpetrated by Tetzel on the people of Wittenberg. Following the punitive response of the papacy, however, he was impelled to consider the wider ramifications of the exchange of 'works' for grace. His personal experience of the inadequacy of penance to liberate him from guilt convinced him that no such equation could legitimately be drawn. As a result, Luther concluded that the entire penitential system of the Catholic Church was nothing more than a systematic and blasphemous confidence trick.

In *The Babylonian Captivity of the Church* (1521) Luther elaborates a detailed critique of the idea that grace can be earned by human actions; an idea which he calls 'works righteousness'. In his opinion, this 'fleshly' mode of thought has polluted virtually every aspect of Catholic doctrine. In the mass, for example, the ceremonial actions of the priest are believed to bring about a 'transubstantiation', exchanging the bread and wine for the body and blood of Christ. In Luther's view, this doctrine perniciously misconstrues the relationship between the material and the spiritual. It suggests that the priest can transform a representation of God into physical reality. According to Luther, the Catholic mass thus fits the Old Testament definition of idolatry; it establishes an illusory equivalence between ideas and matter through the medium of representation, and it does so by fetishizing human activity. This belief in the magical efficacy of the priestly acts is necessary, according to Luther, to enable the priest to sell his labour and perform masses for money. As he puts it in the *Commentary on Galatians*:

> The pope has taken away the true use of the Mass and has simply turned it into merchandise that one must buy for the benefit of another person. There stood the Mass priest at the altar, an apostate who denied Christ and blasphemed the Holy Spirit; and he was doing a work not only for himself but for others, both living and dead, even for the entire church, and that simply by the mere performance of the act.
>
> (XXVI, 135)

It is necessary to conceive of the mass as a miraculous 'work' performed by the priest in order that it may be exchanged for money. Such a belief blasphemously removes salvationary power from Christ's sacrifice and bestows it on a fetishized human act. Throughout his polemical career, Luther dwells on the contention that this fetishization serves the purposes of an ecclesiastical market economy:

> there is no opinion more generally held or more firmly believed in the church today than this, that the mass is a good work and a sacrifice. And this abuse has brought an endless host of other abuses in its train, so that the faith of this sacrament has become wholly extinct and the holy sacrament has been turned into mere merchandise, a market, and a profit-making business. Hence participations, brotherhoods, intercessions, merits, anniversaries, memorial days and the like wares are bought and sold, traded and bartered, in the church. On these the priests and monks depend for their entire livelihood.
>
> (XXXVI, 35–6)

The effect of this 'market' on the minds of the congregation was, according to Luther, to produce an earth-bound, objectified or 'fleshly' consciousness, in which faith is occluded and replaced by a belief in the efficacy of 'works'. The temptation to lapse into this false consciousness is constant for fallen humanity, but Luther believes that a consistent, thoroughgoing awareness of this pernicious tendency will force the believer to place his or her faith in divine agency.

This resistance to the idolatrous fetishization of human works informed the consciousness of Protestant Europe for centuries. For example, in John Bunyan's allegory *The Pilgrim's Progress* (1678), the wayfaring Christian is misdirected by 'Mr Worldly-Wiseman' to seek the counsel of one 'Legality', who dwells in the village of 'Morality'. He discovers his error when 'Evangelist' informs him that Worldly-Wiseman is of a 'carnal temper':

> This Legality therefore is not able to set thee free from thy burden . . . [i.e. of sin]. No man was as yet ever rid of his burden by him, no, nor ever is like to be: ye cannot be justified by the Works of the Law; for by the deeds of the Law no man living can be rid of his burden: therefore Mr. Worldly-Wiseman is an alien, and Mr. Legality a cheat; and for his Son Civility, notwithstanding his simpering looks, he is but a hypocrite, and cannot help thee.[11]

For Luther as for Machiavelli, then, false consciousness occurs when human beings make fetishes of their own deeds. In the arena of secular politics, Machiavelli describes a transformation of established patterns of behaviour, or 'custom', into an immutable 'second nature', and he identifies this manoeuvre as the principal obstacle to innovative government. In the field of theology, Luther finds the root of error in the belief that human actions can save our souls. As we shall see, these criticisms of mortal hubris provide solid foundations for later thinkers, when they set about the tasks of criticizing and dismantling the ecclesiastical and secular institutions of medieval Europe.

In Francis Bacon's *Novum Organon* (1620), the originally religious concept of 'idolatry' is adapted into a fully secular theory of false consciousness. Bacon divides the various kinds of mistaken ideas into four classes of 'idols'. The 'idols of the tribe' refer to the presuppositions and prejudices which enter the mind as a result of living in society. Mere social conventions are taken for eternal verities, and so the products of the mind are mistaken for absolute truths:

> the human understanding is like a false mirror, which, receiving rays irregularly, distorts and discolours the nature of things by mingling its own nature with it.[12]

Since this kind of error results from the intrinsic qualities of human nature, it cannot be altogether avoided. We can, however, guard against it by scrupulously resisting the temptation to idolize our own ideas by arrogantly regarding them as eternal or absolute. The second class of idol, the 'idols of the cave', are the mistakes which arise from the purely personal predilections of individuals; and third, the 'idols of the Market-place' indicate the mental distortions which result from ignorance of the creative power of linguistic representation: 'For men believe that their reason governs words; but it is also true that words react on the understanding' (80). The signs which mediate between ideas and things must therefore be taken into account by any coherent theory of knowledge.

These three kinds of 'idol' Bacon labels 'native', or inherent in the human mind, and he therefore sees them as unavoidable. In contrast, the fourth class, which Bacon terms the 'idols of the theatre', and which includes all closed philosophical systems which try to force empirical reality to accord with their own formal patterns, is termed 'adventitious'. That is to say, these idols are originally extraneous to the mind and they can therefore be expelled. Bacon's division of the idols into two classes anticipates a distinction often found in later discussions of ideology, between those false ideas which arise spontaneously out of everyday social life, and those which are introduced with a degree of calculation, usually with the purpose of perpetuating a particular form of power or control. This distinction became an extremely pressing issue when, in the middle of the seventeenth century, a section of the English nation found itself attempting to replace its ancient system of government by force of arms.

2

EMPIRICISM

Divinity, adieu!
(Marlowe, *Dr Faustus*, I, i, 48)

THE FIRST REVOLUTION

The English Revolution of the mid-seventeenth century was the first modern attempt to reorder the political affairs of an entire nation, while simultaneously reforming the consciousness of its citizens. John Milton, the official propagandist for Cromwell's revolutionary government, was compelled to enlist ancient and medieval ideas in the service of political innovation, just as Machiavelli had done in Renaissance Florence. Specifically, Milton's work employs the Platonic dichotomy between ideal and material spheres, and combines it with the Aristotelian concept of custom to offer an explanation of why people collude in their own oppression. For a time, Milton believed that by purging monarchy and prelacy out of the Commonwealth it might be possible to build a reformed society, and to people it with virtuous citizens. Like most revolutions from above, however, the Cromwellian state soon foundered on the rocks of popular conservatism, and the monarchy was restored in 1660. The revolutionary regime's intellectual apologists were thus faced with the weary task of comprehending 'an inconstant, irrational and Image-doting rabble'.[1] How was it possible to account for people who, as it seemed, voluntarily chose slavery over freedom?

The most readily available explanation was the Christian myth of the Fall, and in *Paradise Lost* Milton undertakes a long meditation on the nature of the postlapsarian mind. Milton's epic endorses the common assumption that Adam and Eve's alienation from God had obscured humanity's *oculus intellectualis*, or 'eye of understanding'. Their posterity is therefore doomed to reverse the Platonic hierarchy, and allow their fleshly appetites to dominate their intellect. As they are being expelled from Eden, Adam and Eve are informed that this mental error will result in political oppression:

> Therefore since hee permits
> Within himself unworthy Powers to reign
> Over free Reason, God in Judgment just
> Subjects him from without to violent Lords;
> Who oft as undeservedly enthral
> His outward freedom.[2]

Paradise Lost represents this false consciousness as a universal human trait, and this doubtless reflects Milton's pessimism after the Restoration. But such a universal false consciousness could not account for the political and religious divisions within the English nation. How could it be that some people were quite able to perceive what Milton took to be the moral and godly way to organize Church and state, while others were so utterly deluded? In the speech quoted above Milton has the archangel Michael inform Adam that mankind is condemned to live under tyranny because 'inordinate desires' and 'upstart Passions' will usurp the place of Reason in the human mind. In *Paradise Lost* these disruptive forces are identified primarily with sensual appetite and undisciplined emotion. However, the work Milton produced during the more hopeful days of the Commonwealth indicates that his understanding of sensuality has a political dimension which extends far beyond any censorious exhortations to an austere personal morality.

In the prose works which Milton composed in his capacity as polemical pamphleteer during the 1640s and 1650s, the Aristotelian notion of custom subtly modifies the Platonic denigration of sensuality. According to Milton 'the prostrate worshippers of Custom'[3] commit idolatry. That is to say, they genuflect before merely human practices and institutions, treating them as if they were divinely ordained and thus immutable. A blind adherence to 'custom' is, in fact, a form of sensuality. Like the pleasures of the flesh, the traditions of man are material, earthly things, and to fetishize them by allowing them to inhibit the free exercise of reason is therefore idolatrous.

Milton's explicitly political conception of the link between custom and idolatry is an important development in the history of ideology. The Scriptural injunction against adoring 'the work of men's hands'[4] could be interpreted as a command that no human traditions, institutions or assumptions should be regarded as sacrosanct. During the crisis of the mid-seventeenth century, the 'idol' or 'tyrant' custom became a topical concern. Meric Casaubon's *A Treatise of Use and Custome* (1638), alludes to the ancient idea that

> custome having once got the strength of long continuance, insinuates errors and impostures (bee they never so grosse) into the minds of most men under the shape and representation of genuine truth: So Justin Martyr; who fetcheth hence especially the origine of Idolatrie.[5]

Milton began his polemical career by applying this idea to the organization of the Church. In *The Reason of Church-Government* (1642) he notes that the Gospel warns against heeding 'the pride and wisdom of the flesh', which 'consists in a bold presumption of ordering the worship and service of God after man's own will in traditions and ceremonies' (I, 826). The episcopal hierarchy and the conducting of services according to conventional 'set forms' are declared to be barriers to the true knowledge of God, on the grounds that they subject His worshippers to merely human traditions.

In the tumultuous 1640s, criticism of the Church could rapidly be extended into other spheres. By 1642 Milton was generalizing from his criticism of the Anglican hierarchy into wider epistemological issues: 'the service of Prelaty', he remarks, 'is perfect slavery, and by consequence perfect falsehood' (I, 853). By the following year, in *The Doctrine and Discipline of Divorce*, he had extended his iconoclasm to the most intimate areas of private conduct. 'The greatest burden in the world,' he writes, 'is superstition; not only of Ceremonies in the Church, but of imaginary and scarecrow sins at home' (II, 228). Arguing for the legalization of divorce on the grounds of mental incompatibility, Milton declares that marriage must no longer be 'worshipt like some Indian deity' (II, 277). Under the pressure of simultaneous upheavals in his personal life[6] and in the political life of the nation, Milton was driven to broaden his originally liturgical attack on idolatry, so that the concept could be applied to any human practice with pretensions to immutability. In *Areopagitica* (1644), Milton arrives at the radical conclusion that truth is necessarily historical: 'Truth is compar'd in Scripture to a streaming fountain; if her waters be not in a perpetuall progression, they sick'n into a muddy pool of conformity and tradition' (II, 543). Innovation is thus to be welcomed, and even when it appears shockingly radical, this can be attributed to our faulty perception: 'our eyes blear'd and dimm'd with prejudice and custom' (II, 565) will be unable to discern new truths.

Milton not only saw that idolatry and custom can deform the mind as well as the institutions of Church and state; he also suggested that there is a causal relationship between external oppression and internal error. In *Areopagitica* he worries lest 'while we still affect by all means a rigid external formality, we may as soon fall again into a gross conforming stupidity' (II, 564), and *The Tenure of Kings and Magistrates* (1650), in which Milton achieves a fully-fledged theory of revolution, opens with a lengthy consideration of how mistaken ideas are linked to political repression:

> If men within themselves would be govern'd by reason, and not generally give up their understanding to a double tyrannie, of Custom from without, and blind affections within, they would discerne better, what it is to favour and uphold the Tyrant of a Nation. But being slaves within doors, no wonder that they strive so much to have the public State conformably govern'd to the inward vitious rule, by which they govern themselves.
>
> (III, 190)

The regicidal *Eikonoklastes* (1649) makes explicit the connection between the attacks on ecclesiastical and secular government: 'the People, exorbitant and excessive in all their motions, are prone ofttimes not to a religious onely, but to a civil kinde of Idolatry in idolizing their Kings' (III, 343). It seems clear that, for Milton, the sweep of events during the 1640s laid bare the surreptitious workings of tyrannical custom and sensual idolatry throughout the Church, the home, the mind and the state.

The English Revolution, then, produced among its most perspicacious advocates a fairly sophisticated theory of false consciousness. As the above quotation indicates, however, the 'People' straggled some way behind the intellectual vanguard. The ultimate failure of the Revolution would force the issue of systematic error into philosophical prominence. Milton's preoccupation with the Fall and its consequences, exemplified in *Paradise Lost*, was one way of accounting for the tenacity of popular misconception. But, by applying concepts such as 'idolatry' and 'superstition' beyond the religious sphere, Milton had already prepared the way for a thoroughly secularized investigation of ideology.

HOBBES AND THE EMPIRICIST TRADITION

Milton and the other radical 'puritans' of the early modern period insisted that the spiritual dimension of consciousness must be kept free from any taint of materiality – whether this took the form of visible church decoration or ceremony, the dead weight of tradition and custom, or the coercive intervention of the sovereign. The intention behind this argument was to reserve for religion a privileged status which would lie beyond the jurisdiction of the civil power. But this radical separation of material and spiritual competencies was susceptible to a very different interpretation. In Thomas Hobbes's *Leviathan* (1651), the rift between the kingdoms of God and Caesar is presented in such a way as to reduce the religious sphere to practical irrelevance.

Hobbes begins his book by establishing the fundamental difference between objects in the material world, and the ways in which these objects are represented in the human mind. The 'motion' of the external objects 'presseth our organs' so as to produce sense impressions of such qualities as colour and sound. However, these qualities are not inherent in the objects themselves, but are produced by our own sensory perceptions. It therefore follows that 'the object is one thing, the image or fancy is another.'[7] The Platonic incommensurability of spirit and matter is here refracted into an irreconcilable division between the physical world and the concepts which human beings can have of that world.[8] Perception, according to Hobbes, must always be a representation of an object which is not fully knowable in itself. The final section of *Leviathan*, entitled 'Of the Kingdom of Darknesse', suggests that the tendency to fetishize these purely subjective representations is the cause of religious idolatry:

> Before our Saviour preached, it was the generall Religion of the
> Gentiles, to worship for Gods, those Appearances that remain
> in the Brain from the impression of external Bodies upon the
> organs of their Senses, which are commonly called *Ideas,
> Idols, Phantasmes, Conceits*, as being Representations of those
> externall Bodies, which cause them, and have nothing in them
> of reality, no more than the things which seem to stand before
> us in a Dream.
>
> (665)

Here we can perceive how the theological concept of idolatry
mutated into the secular notion of ideology. The idolatry of the
gentiles, says Hobbes, consisted in the worship of their own ideas.
This worship was possible only because the benighted heathens
did not perceive that their ideas were not self-sufficient, but were
caused by external objects and mediated through the faculty of
representation. (With his customary tact, Hobbes refrains from
stating the obvious inference that it is idolatrous for *any* society
to make fetishes of its ideas by regarding them as absolute or
eternal). The antidote to such error would be to point out that all
ideas are determined by material phenomena, and are therefore
contingent upon external circumstances. Hobbes thus advocates a
sceptical materialism calculated to demolish any impious claim to
transcendent truth.

The fact that religion makes just such a claim led Hobbes
conclusively to distinguish theology from philosophy. 'The Scripture',
he declares, 'was written to shew unto men the kingdome of
God . . . leaving the world, and the Philosophy thereof, to the
disputation of men, for the exercising of their naturall Reason'
(145). Like Bacon, Hobbes believed that only this 'reason', which
would operate according to the principles of empirical investigation, was capable of giving insight into the material world.
Metaphysics, including theology, is ignominiously relegated to 'the
Kingdom of Fairies' (370). This latter field of investigation is

harmless enough, if rather irrelevant, unless it presumes to interfere with the civil power, in which case Hobbes believes it enters into 'the Kingdome of Darknesse'. To attempt to obtrude religious notions into the theory of state policy is not just mistaken, it is an act of moral turpitude which is designed to serve the selfish interests of the clerical party.

We are faced here with what later philosophers would refer to as the 'instrumentalization' of reason. Before Hobbes, reason had been directed to an end beyond itself; its purpose had been to know, serve, or praise God. Even Bacon and Milton, who did advocate empirical research, conceived of science as a way to 'repair the ruins of our first parents'[9] and regain the perfect knowledge which was lost after the Fall. In *Leviathan*, on the contrary, reason must strictly limit itself to the material world if it is not to be led astray by the nebulous fancies of mere ideas. Reason thus ceases to have any metaphysical purpose, but is to be exclusively concerned with the investigation of data which can be sensually apprehended.

If Milton can be seen as the symbol of revolutionary England, Hobbes was the philosopher in vogue after the Restoration, particularly among the dissolute court of Charles II. Together with his materialism, this gave him a scandalous reputation as an atheistic, immoral thinker, which is memorably expressed in a popular ballad composed after his death, at a venerable age, in 1679:

> Is Atheist Hobbes then dead? Forbear to cry,
> For whilst he liv'd, he thought he could not die,
>   Or was at least most filthy loath to try . . .
>
> In fine, after a thousand shams and fobs,
>   Ninety years eating, and immortal jobs,
> Here Matter lies – and there's an end of Hobbes.[10]

One way of understanding the difference between Hobbes and Milton would be to look at the ways in which they state the opposition between reason and custom. Milton denigrates custom and advocates reason in order to make knowledge *historical*; he envisages truth as being in 'perpetual progression' once it is freed from the restrictive grip of customary assumptions. Hobbes, on the other hand, appeals to reason over custom in order to make truth *trans*-historical. 'Adherence to Custome', he claims, springs from plain 'Ignorance of the nature of Right and Wrong' (165). Social practices and institutions must thus be judged by rational, rather than historical, criteria. For example, Hobbes refuses to concede that precedent is sufficient warrant for a legal code. In order to be legitimate, the law must be formally set down in a constitution:

> we are not to understand that such Customes have their force, onely from Length of Time; but that they were antiently Lawes. written, or otherwise made known, for the Constitutions, and Statutes of their Soveraigns; and are now Lawes, not by vertue of the Praescription of time, but by the Constitutions of their present Soveraigns.
>
> (315)

This sovereignty was first established, according to *Leviathan*, by means of a contract, or 'covenant' between the members of society. Originally, at least hypothetically, the power of the state draws its legitimacy from a rational agreement. Though Hobbes was a political conservative, his theory implicitly contains an assumption which could, in different hands, be used to justify a revolutionary reordering of habitual behaviour. If power originates in a rational contract, rather than acquiring authority through tradition or custom, then everything we do and believe can be re-evaluated according to the standard of reasonable enquiry, without regard for historical precedent: 'if we will reverence the Age', says Hobbes, 'the Present is the Oldest' (727).

As Hobbes sees it, the false apparitions of metaphysics, which have been inculcated to serve the interests of a priestly caste, are not empirically verifiable, and so can be disregarded by serious secular thinkers. He connects religion and custom to the impulse to worship the imaginations of our own minds. Today we might describe them as 'ideological' modes of thought. However, given the uncompromisingly sceptical attitude Hobbes adopts towards the possibility of objective knowledge, might it not be the case that reason itself has ideological elements? Why might not reason also serve the interests of a particular section of society?[11] Hobbes's empiricism also leaves him vulnerable to the charge of deriving eternal verities about human nature from the specific, observable behaviour of people in his own particular society. Most notably, he assumes that the predatory individualism of nascent capitalism reflects an unavoidable 'state of nature'.

Nevertheless, the potential of rational analysis and empirical investigation for exposing and eliminating customary falsehood gave them great appeal for progressive thinkers for centuries after Hobbes. Most significantly for the history of ideology, *Leviathan* made it seem important to study the ways in which ideas are formed, and to investigate the relation of this process to material circumstances. John Locke's *Essay Concerning Human Understanding* (1689) takes a radically empiricist view of the issue. That is to say, Locke holds that there are no innate ideas, but that all knowledge derives from experience. He divides this latter category into 'sensation' of objective, physical things, and 'reflection' on the subjective workings of our minds:

> Our observation, employed either about external sensible objects, or about the internal operations of our minds, perceived and reflected on by ourselves, is that which supplies our understandings with all the materials of thinking.[12]

It is, therefore, possible to examine and account for the formation of ideas in a fairly precise fashion. It is also possible to judge our theories and concepts according to an absolute standard: any ideas which are not demonstrably derived from experience must be regarded as irrational.

It is a particular concern of Locke's to expel 'faith' from philosophical discussion, for 'If the boundaries be not set between faith and reason, no enthusiasm or extravagancy in religion can be contradicted' (589). Locke alludes here to the radical sects which rose to prominence in the army and among the lower classes during the Civil War and the Interregnum, and which he wants to be able to refute. Their utopian and millenarian ideas were clearly unreasonable, since they did not appeal to empirical evidence, but expressed their hopes and desires in largely metaphysical terms. Locke bundles together all these 'strange opinions and extravagant practices' (589) under the rubric of 'enthusiasm', which he claims abandons reason in favour of 'the ungrounded fancies of a man's own brain' (590).

Locke thus excludes from philosophical discussion a great many of the ideas which were, in fact, held by his contemporaries. English empiricism originates as an aggressive, debunking mode of thought, which is concerned to make a polemical intervention in an urgent debate. Locke's *Essay* appeared in the aftermath of the 'glorious and bloodless revolution' of 1688, which forged a compromise between moderate monarchists and parliamentarians, and his apparently unbiased criteria actually militate strongly in favour of the terms of that settlement.

Once again, then, false consciousness consists in the fetishization of mere ideas. This error can be avoided, according to Locke, by accepting only those ideas which can be derived from empirical circumstances, and judged according to 'that standard of reason which is common to us with all men' (597). Reason is a universal, natural principle by which we can learn the correct way to behave. It remains only to explain why many – or even most – people hold opinions which Locke regards as unreasonable. Several obstacles to the free exercise of reason are identified in the *Essay*. People may be 'hindered from inquiry', either by the demands of labour, or deliberately by 'those whose interest it is to keep them ignorant' (599). They may simply not be clever enough to think rationally, or they may 'fear that an impartial inquiry would not favour those opinions which best suit their prejudices, lives, and designs' (600). Incorrect assumptions may be 'riveted' in the mind 'by long custom and education' (601), which lead the unwary 'to reverence them as sacred things' (602). 'Received hypothesis' (602) and 'predominant passions' (603) may also prevent people from following the dictates of reason. Finally, 'authority', or 'the giving up our assent to the common received opinions, either of our friends or party, neighbourhood or country' (606) is the most powerful force which keeps people in error.

Some of these obstacles to true perception are produced by the internal workings of the mind, while others are imposed on it by external forces. This corresponds to Locke's division of 'experience' into two categories: 'reflection' and 'sensation'. We can have experience of things outside us, and we can also experience the operations of our minds. Thus Locke still maintains an 'ideal' dimension of internal experience which is to be regarded as distinct from the sensual or 'material' encounter with the world around us. This raises the questions which dominate the subsequent history of ideology: does one of these kinds of experience determine the other, and if so, which is which?

THE FRENCH CONNECTION

The most interesting responses to the issues raised by English empiricism came from a loosely associated group of eighteenth-century French thinkers who are usually referred to as the *philosophes*, and whose ideas form the basis of the movement which has become known as the Enlightenment. This is not to say that this movement was confined to France; on the contrary, its major exponents looked to England for political example and philosophical inspiration. But precisely because the Reformation and the revolutions of the seventeenth century had rid England of many obstacles to empirical enquiry, the later English empiricists did not approach their task with the same sense of practical urgency as animated the *philosophes*. The French connection of philosophical enquiry with political reform established a link between theory and practice which pervades all subsequent discussions of ideology.

Whereas Locke's empiricism could be used as a weapon against the 'enthusiasm' of radical Protestant sects, the *philosophes* identified the Catholic Church as the enemy of truth. To counter the claims of the Church, thinkers such as Condillac, Helvetius and Holbach had recourse to a 'sensationalist' reading of Locke. This means that they thought Locke's 'sensation' determined his 'reflection', and that all ideas thus had their source in material experience. This kind of philosophy has therefore become known as materialism. In his *Treatise on the Sensations* (1754), Condillac asks his readers to put themselves in the place of a marble statue, to which he then ascribes, one by one, the various senses. By this means he traces human thought processes to their roots in physical sensation. Elsewhere, Condillac says that his method 'consists in re-ascending to the origin of ideas, in tracing their genealogy'.[13] He claims, in short, that our ideas are always produced by material forces, and he evaluates ideas on the basis of their correspondence with material reality. Thus the soul, for example, has no real (because no material) existence, and all subjective human consciousness is nothing but 'transformed sensation'.

As we have seen, this approach involves a secularized version of the religious critique of idolatry. If an idea is empirically ground-less, if it has no material referent, it is considered ethically harmful to treat it as though it were 'real'. We may note in passing that this kind of materialism seems today rather naive: it takes no account, for example, of the fact that the media of representation, in which our ideas must necessarily be expressed, themselves have a material dimension. Nevertheless, in the France of the *ancien régime*, this 'sensationalism' had a radical influence and a practical impact which philosophy did not attain again until the twentieth century. Following Condillac's injunction to search for the origin of ideas in the material world, Claude Helvetius developed a sociological dimension to the critique of 'prejudices'. Helvetius saw that the proposition that non-material ideas had a real existence served the interests of particular social groups – primarily the clergy, whose power depended on their ability to convince the rest of the population of the objective reality of certain metaphysical concepts. Sensationalism thus became closely associated with anti-clericalism, and the *philosophes* went about their work with Helvetius's injunction to 'pull off their masks'[14] ringing in their ears.

Those most assiduous in this enterprise included Voltaire, whose motto 'Ecrasez l'infâme' ('crush infamy') became the battle-cry of the anti-clerical movement, and Holbach, who took Condillac's materialism to its logical conclusion. One of the first overtly atheist philosophers, Holbach viewed false consciousness as the product of a conspiracy. He was sure that the priests were deliberately and cynically inducing people to believe things which were simply not true. In *The System of Nature* (1770) Holbach declares that all error can be traced to the human tendency to 'deceive themselves by abandoning experience to follow imaginary systems'.[15] The tenacity of Aristotle's description of custom as a second nature is clear in Holbach's assertion that people naturally assume the truth of 'prejudices in which they have been instructed from their infancy; with which habit has familiarized them; and which authority has obliged them to conserve' (84).

It seemed that the grip of systematic illusion could only be weakened through a Baconian re-education of the people, which would be conducted on an empirical basis. Helvetius's slogan 'L'education peut tout' neatly expresses the *philosophes*' desire to tear down inherited and customary ideas and reconstruct consciousness on the basis of rational inquiry. However, this faith in the redemptive power of empirical investigation and rational education contradicts the radical sensationalism which the *philosophes* also espoused. When Holbach claims that

> Man's mode of thinking is necessarily determined by his manner
> of being; it must therefore depend on his natural organization,
> and the modification his system receives independently of his
> will.
>
> (93)

he supposes that our thoughts and beliefs are determined by
external circumstances, which operate on us 'independently' of
our conscious intentions. If that is the case, however, how can he
claim that false ideas are consciously inculcated by scheming
priests, rather than automatically assimilated from experience?
Furthermore, how can he account for the fact that he and his
contemporaries have managed to identify false consciousness at
all? Holbach at once says that thought is determined by sensation,
and that thought can develop independently through education
– that is, without corresponding changes in the material environment. In fact, the *philosophes* in general tend to assume that a
project of re-education would be enough to bring about changes
in society. Such a position is incompatible with their own materialism. It took a real, material cataclysm which surpassed their most
ardent hopes and their worst fears to reveal this contradiction in
their ideas.

ROUSSEAU, REVOLUTION, REFLECTION

The materialism of the *philosophes* thus offered a rather bleak
and monochromatic view of the world. Many found the ideas
of Condillac, Helvetius and Holbach to be, quite literally, soul-
destroying. Fortunately, eighteenth-century France offered an
alternative mode of thought to which such people could turn.
Jean-Jacques Rousseau is often grouped among the *philosophes*,
and he associated and collaborated with many of them. But his
own ideas were in sharp contrast to the cold empiricism of their
projects. As Nietzsche remarked, Rousseau set the Enlightenment
on its head.[16] Another way of putting it would be to say that

Rousseau takes the critical method of the Enlightenment and turns it against itself. As we have seen, thinkers from Hobbes on had judged existing social institutions and practices according to the standard of reason. The capacity for rational thought was held to be innate, or 'natural', to the human race. It is this proposition that Rousseau challenges as a 'metaphysical principle'.[17] In an out-flanking, radicalizing gesture, Rousseau subjects reason itself to the kind of critique which the *philosophes* carried out in its name.

What he discovered, as he says in the *Discourse on the Origin of Inequality* (1755), was that reason is actually completely un-natural. He deduces this from an examination of human 'nature'. Due to the distorting effects of civilization, he suggests, our true nature now exists only inside our minds. Rousseau thus rejects the methodology of the *philosophes*, who claimed that it is the external world which forms our consciousness. 'Let us therefore begin', he says, 'by putting aside all the facts, for they have no bearing on the question' (17). The empirical, materialist approach, which treats the mind as an object, is itself part of the problem it purports to remedy: 'it is by dint of studying man that we have rendered ourselves incapable of knowing him' (11). By examining his own subjective nature, Rousseau evolves the hypothetical concept of the 'state of nature', which he uses as a standard against which to judge contemporary society. Taking issue with Hobbes's description of this condition as ethically inferior to civilization, Rousseau claims that moral categories do not apply to pre-social beings: 'savages are not evil precisely because they do not know what it is to be good' (36). Hobbes has 'wrongly injected into the savage man's concern for self-preservation the need to satisfy a multitude of passions which are the product of society' (35).

In the late eighteenth century, Rousseau's ideas spawned the philosophical and literary movement known as Romanticism. The Romantics revolted against the social and aesthetic consequences of burgeoning industrial capitalism, and advocated a return to what they imagined had been more 'natural' ways of living and thinking. In William Wordsworth's preface to the *Lyrical Ballads* (1800), the poet explains his choice of mainly rural themes in Rousseau-esque tones:

> Humble and rustic life was generally chosen, because in that condition, the essential passions of the heart find a better soil in which they can attain their maturity, are under less restraint, and speak a plainer and more emphatic language ... in that condition the passions of men are incorporated with the beautiful and permanent forms of nature.[18]

Along with the advocacy of the pastoral goes an appeal to 'passion', and a mistrust and denigration of 'reason' as an unnatural mode of thought. Reason, for Rousseau, is the faculty which has tempted man to abandon the state of nature and become civilized. It is thus a decidedly dubious quality:

> I almost dare to affirm that the state of reflection is a state contrary to nature and that the man who meditates is a depraved animal. ... Reason is what engenders egocentrism, and reflection strengthens it. Reason is what turns man in upon himself. Reason is what separates him from all that troubles and afflicts him.

(37)

This latter freedom from animalistic fears, while apparently comforting, is not achieved without cost. In Rousseau's words, people are led 'to buy imaginary repose at the price of real felicity' (17). As human beings begin to combine in societies, their natural differences in strength and ability become perverted into inequality (53). Private property is the foundation of all inequality (44), and is the most unnatural institution of all. Once the principle of social hierarchy has been established, moreover, people will distort and deny their true natures in order to enhance their social status, so that 'Being something and appearing to be something become two completely different things' (54). The result is that people are no longer able to perceive the natural equality which lies behind the surface inequalities of civilization. Rousseau's major contribution to the history of ideology was to see that this pervasive ignorance was instituted to protect the interests of property holders:

> the rich, pressed by necessity, finally conceived the most thought-out project which ever entered the human mind. It was to use in his favor the very strength of those who attacked him, to turn his adversaries into his defenders, to instill in them other maxims, and to give them other institutions which were as favorable to him as natural right was unfavorable to him.
>
> (56)

Thus the whole apparatus of civilized society has the purpose of maintaining an eminently unnatural division of wealth. An appeal to reason as a way of judging social institutions, such as was made by the empiricist *philosophes*, fails to recognize that reason is itself an unnatural, or social, phenomenon, and that it is thus part of the problem to which it purports to be a solution. In place of this artificial standard, Rousseau proposes a new one: the 'state of nature'. As with Hobbes, it must be stressed that this is not intended as more than a hypothetical postulate which can be used to reveal the arbitrary status of present social relations. In fact, Rousseau's appeal to nature amounts, in practice, to an appeal to history:

> In discovering and following thus the forgotten and lost routes that must have led man from the natural state to the civil state ... no attentive reader can fail to be struck by the immense space that separates these two states. It is in this slow succession of things that he will see the solution to an infinity of moral and political problems which the philosophers are unable to resolve ... he will explain how the soul and human passions

are imperceptibly altered and, as it were, change their nature; why, in the long run, our needs and passions change their objects; why, with original man gradually disappearing, society no longer offers to the eyes of the wise man anything but an assemblage of artificial men and factitious passions which are the work of these new relations and have no true foundation in nature.

(69)

Here the originally religious injunction against fetishizing our own 'works' is used to expose the 'artificial men' of civilized society. The empiricists had rejected any metaphysical concepts on the grounds that they are not 'real', but rather human inventions. Rousseau goes a step further, pointing out that *all* social practices, including reason itself, are human inventions. In the hands of his followers, Rousseau's Romanticism frequently involves an open revolt against rationality and an appeal for humanity to return to a more 'natural' mode of inner experience. This tendency culminates in such irrationalist expostulations as John Keats's demand in 1817, 'for a Life of Sensations rather than of Thoughts!'[19] Because all rational social conventions and traditions are man-made, there is a sense in which they are not 'real' – there is nothing natural, eternal or inevitable about them. Everything, therefore, can be changed.

The empiricist *philosophes* also wanted to change things. But they envisaged a gradual, Baconian process of re-education, which would tactfully remove the idols and install reason in their place. Despite the obstruction of the *ancien régime* in Church and state, this philosophical project was making modest but significant progress in Enlightenment France. Rousseau's iconoclasm was much more radical; in fact, it was revolutionary. It is hardly surprising that it was Rousseau rather than Condillac who was heralded as a prophet by the radical Jacobins, or that Robespierre insisted that a cult of the Rousseauian 'Supreme Being' replace what he called the 'ridiculous farces' celebrating deified Reason.[20] Rather than

implying rational reform, Rousseau's theories suggested the possibility of wiping away the entire structure of social organization and
starting anew. As the French revolutionary constitution of 1791
declared, 'there is no longer any nobility nor peerage nor hereditary
distinctions of orders nor feudal regime nor patrimonial justice
nor any title, denomination or prerogative.'[21]

The Constituent Assembly thus established the formal equality
of all men. Even before the constitution was completed, however,
this notion had been the subject of a devastating critique by the
Anglo-Irish politician Edmund Burke. In his *Reflections on the
Revolution in France* (1790), Burke claimed that the revolutionaries
had misread their purported mentor. 'I believe', he declared, 'that
were Rousseau alive, and in one of his lucid intervals, he would
be shocked at the practical phrenzy of his scholars.'[22] In Burke's
opinion, Rousseau had been making essentially philosophical
arguments and did not intend that anyone should attempt to
put them into practice, for the very good reason that this was
impossible. Social institutions, in Burke's view, are historically
determined, and it is therefore the ultimate in 'presumption' to
regard society as a *carte blanche*, to be restructured at will:

> as the liberties and the restrictions vary with times and cir-
> cumstances, and admit of infinite modifications, they cannot
> be settled upon any abstract rule; and nothing is so foolish as
> to discuss them upon that principle.
>
> (72)

The revolutionaries' error was to have assumed that Rousseau's
'state of nature' was an empirically attainable condition, rather
than a hypothetical postulate designed to make us evaluate our
customs historically. Rousseau says that people are by nature
equal, and the revolutionaries are thereby led to assert something
that is manifestly empirically not the case – that all men are equal
here and now. This, as Burke saw, is a purely formal equality, with
no material reality:

Believe me, Sir, those who attempt to level, never equalize [they] only change and pervert the natural order of things; they load the edifice of society, by setting up in the air what the solidity of the structure requires to be on the ground.

(57–8)

What Burke calls the 'metaphysic rights' of man (73) are, in reality, not universal at all: rather, they are a mask (we might say an ideology) disguising sectional interests:

The whole of the power obtained by this revolution will settle in the towns among the burghers, and the monied directors who lead them. . . . Here end all the deceitful dreams and visions of the equality and rights of men. In 'the Serbonian bog' of this base oligarchy they are all absorbed, sunk, and lost for ever.

(240, 242)

Thus the mere assertion that men are, in the abstract, 'equal', unaccompanied by any attempt to make them equal in fact, is identified by Burke as bourgeois ideology. The 'monied interest' requires this formal equality – the removal of all obstacles to the free pursuit of wealth and power – for its own ends, but it cunningly claims to be following a universal principle and restoring society to a 'natural' condition.

With admirable perspicuity, Burke foresaw the consequences of this desire to erase the work of history, and to cut away the 'false' accoutrements of culture and tradition. Any attempt to realize Rousseau's 'state of nature' in practice could only reduce humanity to the condition of Tom O' Bedlam:

All the super-added ideas, furnished from the wardrobe of a moral imagination, which the heart owns, and the understanding ratifies, as necessary to cover the defects of our naked shivering nature, and to raise it to dignity in our own estimation, are to be exploded as a ridiculous, absurd, and antiquated fashion.

> On this scheme of things, a king is but a man; a queen is but
> a woman; a woman is but an animal; and an animal not of the
> highest order.
>
> (92–3)

As Shakespeare puts it in *King Lear*, 'Allow not nature more
than nature needs/ Man's life is cheap as beast's' (II, iv, 266–7).[23]
The 'natural' state to which the revolutionaries wanted to restore
France would, as Burke foresaw, resemble that of Hobbes far more
closely than that of Rousseau. After the dust of the revolution had
settled, however, important achievements remained. One was the
elevation of the universalizing, naturalizing, equalizing ideology
of the bourgeoisie to something approaching orthodoxy, in
which position it remains, by and large, to this day. Another,
which is perhaps a result of the former, was the establishment in
a prominent place among the human sciences of the study of
'ideology'.

DESTUTT DE TRACY AND THE INVENTION
OF IDEOLOGY

One of the many replies to Burke's attack on the French
Revolution came from a renegade aristocrat and member of the
revolutionary Constituent Assembly named Destutt de Tracy. In a
fifteen-page pamphlet of 1790, Destutt took issue with Burke's
advocacy of the moderate, compromising English settlement of
1688 as a model for France. This was no time for half measures, he
claimed, what was needed was a 'complete revolution'.[24] Six years
later, as a member of the Institut de France, Destutt invented the
term 'ideology', and sixteen years after that Napoleon Bonaparte
did him the honour of blaming him for the retreat from Moscow,
as well as for the revolutionary Terror:

> We must lay the blame for the ills which our fair France has
> suffered on ideology, that shadowy metaphysics which subtly

searches for first causes on which to base the legislation of
peoples, rather than making use of the laws known to the
human heart and of the lessons of history. These errors must
inevitably and did in fact lead to the rule of bloodthirsty men.[25]

On a personal level, the accusation was most unfair; Destutt had
actually been imprisoned under the Terror, and only Thermidor
saved him from the guillotine. But Napoleon was correct to ascribe
a dangerous, radical and destructive tendency to the science of
'ideology' which Destutt invented.

Bonaparte pointed out that Destutt's 'ideology' neglects to
examine 'the laws known to the human heart and of the lessons of
history'. As he says, this science reacts against both the idealist
notion of *a priori* concepts, and the possibility of historical
determinism. These reactions bespeak the legacy of Locke and
Condillac, the two most important influences on Destutt's
thought. His reading of these thinkers led him to believe, as he says
in the *Elemens d'Idéologie* (1804–15), that there were no innate
ideas, all thought being derived from sensation. On the other
hand, he also thought that 'Nothing exists for us except by the
ideas we have of it, because our ideas are our whole being, our
existence itself.'[26] As with Hobbes, things create ideas, but these
ideas can never be fully adequate to the things. The only way to
avoid the sceptical position that true knowledge is impossible, so it
seemed to Destutt, would be to analyse the process by which our
minds translate material things into ideal forms. This area of study
had already been opened up by Condillac; under the leadership of
Destutt it was institutionalized in the section of the Institut de
France which dealt with moral and political sciences, and it was
given the name 'Idéologie': the science of ideas.

Ideology thus originates as a 'meta-science', a science of science.
It claims to be able to explain where the other sciences come from,
and to give a scientific genealogy of thought. As Napoleon came to
recognize, this amounted to a claim to superiority over all other

disciplines, and by his vigorous suppression of the *idéologues* after 1803 he acknowledged the threat posed by this hubristic science to his own despotic ambition. Napoleon's plans called for the imposition of an ideology in the derogatory sense of the term: he thought, for example, that Christianity could ensure 'public order'. The project of the *idéologues* threatened to 'destroy all illusions'[27] and thus unmask the base designs behind the Emperor's embrace of the Vatican.

Destutt de Tracy's 'ideology', then, traces ideas, through sensations, to their roots in matter. But this science moves beyond Condillac's reductive materialism by emphasizing more strongly the movement, the process through which human beings interact with their material surroundings. Destutt was thus able to claim that 'Idéologie' achieves a momentous philosophical break-through, by transcending the ancient oppositions between matter and spirit, things and concepts. He is therefore led, as Emmet Kennedy observes, 'in two opposite directions – towards an idealist conception of error and a sensationalist conception of truth.'[28] That is to say, while the sensations we get from external objects are reliable and accurate, the ideas which these sensations produce in our minds may be wrongly arranged, and so lead us to false conclusions. By observing the movement by which sensations are transformed into ideas, it ought to be possible to understand, and so to avoid, the ways in which such erroneous patterns of ideas come into being.

The new discipline of 'ideology', then, claimed to be nothing less than the science to explain all sciences. It had ambitions to establish 'a grammar and language modeled after mathematics . . . in which each idea was assigned its corresponding linguistic sign.'[29] This system could then be used to study the relations between ideas, as well as to identify their origins. As Napoleon understood, however, the practical implications of such a science meant that it could not itself be disinterested. To 'unmask' the source of ideas was to deny them absolute validity. If this was to be done to all ideas, it was easy to see how Destutt's ambition to 'change the face of the earth'[30] might seem plausible enough. Unfortunately for him, Destutt de Tracy was not the only man in France with such ambitions. Napoleon recognized a threat when he saw one; he was also shrewd enough to perceive that 'Idéologie' involved a thoroughgoing scepticism towards all authoritative knowledge, which must issue in continual chaos and 'lead to the rule of bloodthirsty men'.

It would thus be wrong to see, in the unequal struggle between the *idéologues* and Bonaparte, a symbol of the contradictory demands of theory and practice. When he attacked Destutt and his followers as 'dreamers' and 'windbags', Napoleon did not suggest that their theories were purely 'ideal', with no bearing on political reality. On the contrary, he knew that their theories were all too relevant to political issues. If they were allowed to pursue their millennial aims, he foresaw a permanent revolution: a maelstrom in which ideas were continually being unmasked, invalidated and replaced by new ones. The subsequent history of ideology and its relations with practical politics would seem to bear him out.

3

IDEALISM

What you call the Spirit of the Age
Is in reality the spirit of those men
In which their time's reflected.

(Goethe, *Faust*, 577–9)[1]

DESCARTES'S EGO

During the seventeenth and eighteenth centuries, empiricism and materialism provided a rational basis for the study of consciousness. This allowed 'Idéologie' to take its place among the sciences of the Enlightenment. But in the process of analysing the formation of ideas, the *idéologues* deprived this process of the dignity and reverence to which it had previously seemed entitled. In particular, the concept of the soul could have no place in the materialism of the *philosophes*. Destutt de Tracy's remark that 'Idéologie' was a branch of zoology evinced a rather cavalier attitude to the cherished notion that there is some kind of supernatural, quasi-divine essence within the mind which elevates humanity above the animals. Rousseau provided one escape route for those whose sensibilities were too delicate to countenance studying the mind like any other object of science. But Rousseau wrote in direct reaction to the doctrines of materialism, and his glorification of the autonomous, individual self is merely the reverse side, the antithesis, of Condillac and Destutt's dour sensationalism. For a more rational and coherent account of the mind's freedom from matter, it is necessary to return to the seventeenth century, to the work of René Descartes.

When, in *The Sufferings of Young Werther* (1774), Goethe has his protagonist announce that 'I return into myself, and find a world!',[2] he reacts against the 'sensationalist' doctrine that all mental processes can be traced to external stimuli. Descartes also finds a superior ground for certainty within the individual self, or subject. In his early tract *Rules for the Direction of our Intelligence* (1628), Descartes unequivocally declares that 'the human mind has something within it that we may call divine, wherein are scattered the first germs of useful modes of thought.'[3] This assumption is radically at odds with the materialist project of tracing the origin of human ideas to causes in the external world. Descartes notes that our senses, through which we inevitably experience material things, can often deceive us. A tower which appears round when viewed from one angle may appear square from another; when dreaming or in a delusional condition we may think we see objects which are not there, and so on. Descartes thus believes that 'prejudices' arise from putting too much credence in what we naively assume to be our experience of the world outside us, which is in fact mediated through our notoriously unreliable senses. In the *Meditations on First Philosophy* (1641), Descartes notes the problematic status of sense-perception, and consequently advocates 'doubt about all things and especially about material things' (140). Such a systematic doubt is useful 'inasmuch as it delivers us from every kind of prejudice, and sets out for us a very simple way by which the mind may detach itself from the senses.' In fact, the only thing of which the mind can be absolutely certain is the existence of its own activity. Descartes expressed this claim in the famous aphorism *cogito ergo sum*, 'I think therefore I am.'[4]

Descartes intends this as a self-confirming proposition. That is, he believes that its truth is established in the very act of conceiving it. However, on closer examination we can see that this is not quite so. The so-called '*cogito*' certainly proves that thought exists. But Descartes draws from this the unwarranted conclusion that there also exists an individual, unified subject – an 'I' – which is doing the thinking. From this presupposition Descartes proposes to deduce the rest of his theory. The originary, unitary, transcendent Cartesian ego thus provides an alternative standard of certainty and coherence for a world in which the traditional conception of God as the source of all truth was rapidly being diminished.

Since he will admit the certainty only of his own self and its thought-processes, Descartes assumes an irreconcilable divergence, or dualism, between the material world and the ideas we have about that world. This is the most important difference between Descartes and the materialists. Descartes does not believe that thought derives from sensation – that it is, as Condillac was to put it, 'transformed sensation'. Rather, he insists on the separation between the ideal and material spheres. Because he believes that our innate rational capacities determine and make possible our experience of the world, Descartes is usually referred to as a rationalist. In the third *Meditation*, Descartes claims that we do not really perceive the external world at all:

I have before received and admitted many things to be very certain and manifest, which yet I afterwards recognized as being dubious. What then were these things? They were the earth, sky, stars and all other objects which I apprehended by means of the senses. But what did I clearly and distinctly perceive in them? Nothing more than that the ideas or thoughts of these things were presented to my mind. And not even now do I deny that these ideas are met with in me. But

IDEALISM 61

there was yet another thing which I affirmed, and which, owing to the habit which I had formed of believing it, I thought I perceived very clearly, although in truth I did not perceive it at all, to wit, that there were objects outside of me from which these ideas proceeded, and to which they were entirely similar.

(158)

When we think we are seeing objects in the material world, we are really seeing only our ideas, or concepts, of objects which may or may not exist outside us. Ignorance of this fact is the prime cause of false consciousness: 'the principal error and the commonest . . . consists in my judging that the ideas which are in me are similar or conformable to the things outside me' (160). As we saw in the previous chapter, empiricists such as Hobbes also argue that the material world is incommensurable with our ideas of it. For Hobbes, however, this means that we should strive all the harder to verify our concepts with reference to material reality, even in the knowledge that the one can never be fully adequate to the other. When an idea becomes so divorced from the empirical that it has no material referent whatsoever, it is liable to be exiled to Hobbes's 'Kingdom of Fairies'. In contrast, Descartes does not believe that ideas must aspire to correspondence with anything 'outside' themselves in order to be valid. Rather than being simply nonsensical, ideas which cannot be traced to empirical things must have another cause, which is not the less real for not being material:

For if we imagine that something is found in an idea which is not found in the cause, it must then have been derived from nought; but however imperfect may be this mode of being by which a thing is objectively or by representation in the understanding by its idea, we cannot certainly say that this mode of being is nothing, nor, consequently, that the idea derives its origin from nothing.

(163)

Our concepts, which are all that we can know, are not necessarily prompted by anything material, but can have a perfectly legitimate ideal origin. Descartes would thus disagree with Locke's comparison of non-material ideas to religious idols. On the contrary, he is of the opinion that our knowledge of ideas is prior to, and more certain than, any knowledge we can have of things in themselves.

'RAVING WITH REASON': KANT AND ENLIGHTENMENT

Descartes's relevance to an account of ideology lies in his claim that our sense-perceptions represent the material world to us in a way that is comprehensively false. There is thus an absolute divergence between reality and our ideas, the 'object' and the 'subject'. We should note that this opposition is mutually defining: the category of 'subject' would have no content without the category of 'object', and vice versa. Nevertheless, the Cartesian dualism provides the basis for the terminology which is conventionally applied to philosophical history. Very broadly, those thinkers, such as Hobbes, who believe that the external world determines our ideas, are known as 'empiricists', and those like Descartes, who believe that our innate ideas form the basis of our experience of reality, are called 'rationalists'. Those, such as Plato, who consider the realm of ideas to be the only true reality are termed 'idealists', and those, like Condillac, who claim that the physical world is more authentic than human concepts are known as 'materialists'. In fact, however, the most interesting philosophers of the three centuries following Descartes are those who tried to overcome or reconcile these fundamental oppositions.

The empiricist approach to this problem was taken to divergent, but equally startling, extremes by two philosophers from the 'Celtic Fringe' of Europe: George Berkeley and David Hume. In *The Dialogue of Hylas and Philonous* (1713), the Irishman Berkeley suggested that we do not have any innate ideas. The only knowledge we can have of the material world comes from our sense-impressions. But we have no reason to believe that these impressions give us an accurate representation of whatever, if anything, may cause them. It follows that, for all practical purposes, the true nature of the external world is unknowable, and things only exist insofar as they are perceived. In fact, objects would cease to exist when unobserved by human beings, were it not for the omnipresence of an observing divinity. Ronald Knox parodied this doctrine in a famous pair of limericks:

> There was a young man who said, 'God
>> Must think it exceedingly odd
>>> If he finds that this tree
>>>> Continues to be
> When there's no-one about in the Quad.'

>> Reply

> 'Dear Sir: Your astonishment's odd:
>> I am always about in the Quad.
>>> And that's why the tree
>>>> Will continue to be,
> Since observed by, yours faithfully, God.'[5]

For the Scottish philosopher David Hume, Berkeley's theory led to the conclusion that our ideas do not correspond to any objective reality, but are merely faint and blurred representations of our physical sense-impressions. Complex ideas are merely combinations of these representations. In his *Treatise of Human Nature* (1739–40), Hume went so far as to claim that, since we have no sensual impression of our own unified self – of what we would today call the 'subject' – we have no knowable internal personality, and are in fact nothing but a bundle of random perceptions, on which we arbitrarily impose an ideal order and label it our 'self'.

The implications of Hume's ideas were extremely radical and disconcerting. Among other things, he neatly eliminated the soul from philosophical consideration: to all intents and purposes it could be regarded as a fiction. Even the consolation of Descartes's unified thinking subject was denied. Moreover, Hume suggested that accurate knowledge of the external world was impossible. The inference could be drawn that we have no reliable criteria for distinguishing truth from falsehood. Even the relation of cause-and-effect was held to be an artificial imposition on a recalcitrant reality. As we shall see, these doctrines of Hume anticipate to a remarkable degree many of the axioms of the twentieth-century postmodernists.[6]

Among those who found these doctrines intolerable was Immanuel Kant, who famously remarked that reading Hume awoke him from his 'dogmatic slumbers' – that is to say, from his uncritical rationalism. In *The Critique of Pure Reason* (1781), Kant takes upon himself the task of establishing beyond all doubt the existence of a transcendent human subject. In other words, he is concerned to demonstrate that we possess a continuous and coherent self, which transcends the random blur of representation. Kant does this by challenging the dualism between rationalism and empiricism. As he says in the introduction:

> though all our knowledge begins with experience, it by no means follows, that all arises out of experience. For, on the contrary, it is quite possible that our empirical knowledge is a compound of that which we receive through impressions, and that which the faculty of cognition supplies from itself.[7]

We are intuitively aware of the objective world outside ourselves, but we can only become truly conscious of that world by unifying these intuitions in the form of concepts. When, for instance, I subsume this objective piece of lead and wood under the ideal, general category of 'pencil', I impose a human concept on a material object, and thus arrive at a properly human knowledge of it. This ability to conceptualize is an innate property of the human understanding.

In place of the rigid Cartesian opposition, Kant thus proposes a unity, whereby knowledge is produced by experience and reason working together. He calls the part of our knowledge which derives from experience 'a posteriori' knowledge, and he refers to knowledge which is logically prior to experience as 'a priori'. This latter field is further divided into 'analytic' and 'synthetic' propositions. The first of these are statements of which the truth is guaranteed by virtue of the predicate being contained in the subject, such as 'the big house is a house'. The second describes statements in which the predicate goes beyond, or adds something to, the subject, such as 'the big house is empty'. In the empiricist view of things, all synthetic judgements must be a posteriori, or derived from experience. Kant, on the other hand, believed that there are certain synthetic judgements which are true a priori, and precede any possible experience. Newtonian science and geometry appeared to offer examples of this kind of judgement. Because their axioms would necessarily be true for any conceivable human experience, they cannot be derived from experience, but must be prior to it. The question which empiricism cannot answer, and which Kant undertakes to answer himself, is thus: how are these synthetic a priori judgements possible?

Kant's answer was that there are, inherent in the human mind, certain 'categories', or ideas which are not empirical, but which make experience possible. Without such concepts as substance and causality, for example, it would simply be impossible to have any kind of recognizably human experience. These categories are therefore not derived from experience, but must spring from some subject which transcends the material. In a sense, Kant is saying that our experience of the material world is made possible – and that the material world is thus, in effect, created 'for us' – by this transcendent subject. This is Kant's 'Copernican revolution'; he suggests that our knowledge need not conform to external objects but that, insofar as we can know them, these objects must conform to our capacity for knowledge. If, as Hume suggests, we do not perceive the object in itself but only as it is mediated through our faculty of intuition then, claims Kant, the object can be known by studying that faculty. The study of the subject can reveal the nature of the object, insofar as it has a nature 'for us'.

Kant agrees that, as Hume argued, we do not perceive the material world as it really is 'in itself'. But by rescuing the subject from Hume's scepticism, Kant shows that it is nevertheless possible to perceive an objective, determinate representation of things. The transcendent subject guarantees our access to absolute truth, even though this truth is only absolute 'for us': that is, from a particular perspective within space and time. Kant thus posits a radical disjunction between the object as it appears to us, and the 'thing-in-itself', of which we can have no knowledge. The realm of our experience is that of 'phenomena', and it has its own coherence and objectivity. This does not mean, however, that it pretends to discover perspectiveless or 'unconditioned' truths about objects in themselves: these belong to the sphere of 'noumena', which exists beyond the ken of human perception. There is a sense in which, as an abstract ideal, this noumenal sphere enables and determines the phenomenal, but we cannot gain access to it through either empirical observation or rational analysis.

It is important to remember that the distinction between the appearance of the thing and the thing-in-itself does not refer to different objects, but to the same object viewed from different perspectives. As appearance, or 'for us', the thing is knowable; but the same thing has another existence 'in itself', of which we can do no more than deduce the possibility. Kant thus theorizes and schematizes to an unsurpassed degree the belief that what we perceive in the world is systematically distinct from the world as it 'really' is. He therefore denounces any hubristic attempt to pronounce on things-in-themselves by removing them from their empirical situation – a tenacious tendency which is labelled 'hypo-statization'. This tendency, Kant feels, is the primary source of false consciousness. However, the human mind is ineluctably drawn to such futile speculation about noumena. The most we can do to avoid this pitfall is to remember always that our knowledge emanates from our perspective: it is inextricably situated in time and space, and we must try to resist the temptation to view our own ideas as though they were absolute or eternal. In this proscription, then, we can make out the echoes of the theological denunciations of idolatry which we discussed in previous chapters.

THE IDEOLOGY OF THE AESTHETIC

The Kantian reaction against empiricism had especially exciting implications for aesthetic theory. In England, Condillac's position that thoughts were simply the result of material, mechanical processes had been espoused and modified by David Hartley, who held that thinking was the result of an original physical stimulus, followed by an automatic process of association of ideas. The Romantic poets William Wordsworth and Samuel Taylor Coleridge were at first impressed with Hartley's theory, but Coleridge later came to find it too soulless and mechanistic for his taste. He circumvented this problem by differentiating, in the *Biographia Literaria* (1817) between two separate mental faculties, which he called the Fancy and the Imagination.[8] The former corresponds to the Hartleyean account of mental processes, which have 'no other counters to play with but fixities and definites' (202). The latter, subdivided into an originary 'primary' and a consequent 'secondary' form, is by contrast an active, creative agency through which the subject imposes itself on the objective world around it.

The philosophical differences between materialist empiricism and subjective idealism can be illustrated by examining two poetic approaches to the same issue: the difficulty of ageing, with its concurrent loss of the passion and inspiration of youth. In the ode entitled 'Intimations of Immortality', Wordsworth laments 'That there hath past away a glory from the earth',[9] and that he no longer experiences the same 'visionary gleam' which illuminated his younger days. The problem is here conceived as resulting from an inevitable process: as one gets older, the intensity of experience which is spontaneously felt by children gradually fades, until 'At length the Man perceives it die away,/ And fade into the light of common day' (75–6). Inspiration is a one-way street, flowing from external nature into the self. At first, this is a tremendously thrilling and wonderful experience, but it loses its lustre as one grows accustomed to it. In 'Dejection: An Ode', his answer to Wordsworth's poem, Coleridge takes issue with his friend's diagnosis of this melancholia:

> I may not hope from outward forms to win
> The passion and the life, whose fountains are within.
>
> O Wordsworth! we receive but what we give,
> And in our life alone does Nature live
>
> (ll.45–8)[10]

Courageously, Coleridge refuses himself the Wordsworthian consolation that the incremental loss of wonder is an ineluctable consequence of a growing familiarity with the external world. Rather, the source of the problem is located within the subject itself. The 'glory and the dream' whose departure is lamented by Wordsworth were always located within the subject, rather than in our objective surroundings, and their loss must therefore indicate an interior problem with the self. We could thus say that the philosophical positions espoused in Wordsworth's and Coleridge's odes are materialist and idealist, respectively.

Kant also addressed the issue of aesthetics in his late work, the *Critique of Judgment* (1790). In the introduction to this text, Kant announces that he is unhappy with the duality, which informs his earlier work, between the phenomenal, or 'sensible', and the 'supersensible' noumenal spheres:

> an immense gulf is fixed between the domain of the concept of nature, the sensible, and the domain of the concept of freedom,

> the supersensible, so that no transition from the sensible to the supersensible . . . is possible, just as if they were two different worlds, the first of which cannot have any influence on the second; and yet the second *is* to have an influence on the first, i.e. the concept of freedom is to actualize in the world of sense the purpose enjoined by its laws. . . . So there must after all be a basis *uniting* the supersensible that underlies nature and the supersensible that the concept of freedom contains practically.[11]

The first kind of 'supersensible' is the noumenon, or thing-in-itself; the second is the 'categorical imperative', or abstract rule which determines ethical behaviour and which, in the *Critique of Practical Reason* (1786) Kant derives from the biblical injunction to do unto others as you would have them do unto you. Because it will result in action, this latter supersensible commandment will transform the material world, or 'actualize in the world of sense the purpose enjoined by its laws'. Thus, there clearly must be some point of connection between the material and the supersensible spheres. The faculty which Kant believes can mediate between these two is that of aesthetic judgement. Kant states the complex relations between the various mental faculties under discussion as follows: 'between the cognitive power and the power of desire lies the feeling of pleasure, just as judgment lies between understanding and reason' (17). What is pleasurable in the contemplation of beauty is the judgement's perception in the object of a 'purposiveness' which is analogous to its own ability to impose concepts on intuitions.

This feeling of pleasure is entirely subjective. On the other hand, it is a feeling which is universally experienced and communicable. This subjective universality is produced, according to Kant, by the interaction or 'free play' of the imagination and the understanding, which can be presumed to operate in all humans, and which is set in motion by the pleasurable object:

the cognitive powers brought into play by this presentation[12] are in free play, because no determinate concept restricts them to a particular rule of cognition. Hence the mental state in this presentation must be a feeling, accompanying the given presentation, of a free play of the presentational powers directed to cognition in general . . . hence this subjective universal communicability can be nothing but [that of] the mental state in which we are when imagination and understanding are in free play [insofar as they harmonize with each other as required for *cognition in general*].

(62)

So the faculty which Kant intends to mediate between his ethics and his epistemology turns out to be nothing but the 'free play' of the mind when confronted by the 'abyss' (115) of a pleasurable representation. It is hardly an entity in itself, but consists in an oscillation between understanding and imagination. What is more, the experience of what Kant calls the 'sublime' further emphasizes the gulf between pure and practical reason – that is, between the ability to conceptualize objects and the ability to act ethically in the world.[13] For Kant, however, the point is not so much the existence of this gulf as the desire to bridge it, which is also provoked by the contemplation of the sublime. Once again, this quality is conceived as existing only within the mind:

nothing that can be an object of the senses is to be called sublime. [What happens is that] our imagination strives to progress toward infinity, while our reason demands absolute totality as a real idea, and so [the imagination,] our power of estimating the magnitude of things in the world of sense, is inadequate to that idea. Yet this inadequacy itself is the arousal in us of the feeling that we have within us a supersensible power. . . . *Sublime is what even to be able to think proves that the mind has a power surpassing any standard of sense.*

(106)

By bringing home to us the gap between our phenomenal perception and the noumenal reality which underlies appearances, the sublime provokes the desire (which must however remain unfulfilled) to achieve access to this 'supersensible' dimension. The effect of the sublime is to drive us toward the two elements of reality we can never grasp: the thing-in-itself, and the totality of existence. The striving after these two unreachable targets is the experience of the sublime:

> to be able even to think the infinite *as a whole* indicates a mental power that surpasses any standard of sense. . . . If the human mind is nonetheless to *be able even to think* the given infinite without contradiction, it must have within itself a power that is supersensible, whose idea of a noumenon cannot be intuited but can yet be regarded as the substrate underlying what is mere appearance, namely, our intuition of the world.
>
> (111)

It is, then, a notable feature of this *Critique* that Kant suggests that the impulse towards the noumena is simultaneously a striving after 'totality'. It is not hard to discern a quasi-religious motive behind this desire for an ultimate, unified reality lying beneath the disparate surface appearances of things. Kant is heavily influenced here by the Protestant proscription of idolatry, and the biblical injunction to eschew the worship of 'the works of men's hands'. For the sublime is that desire which refuses to be satisfied by anything material. Kant is perfectly explicit about the potential of the sublime as an iconoclastic force:

> Perhaps the most sublime passage in the Jewish law is the commandment: Thou shalt not make unto thee any graven image, or any likeness of any thing that is in heaven or on earth, or under the earth, etc. This commandment alone can explain the enthusiasm that the Jewish people in its civilized era felt for

its religion when it compared itself with other peoples, or can explain the pride which Islam inspires.

(135)

Most germane for our purposes is Kant's connection of idolatry with political oppression. Continuing his discussion of graven images, he declares:

> That is also why governments have gladly permitted religion to be amply furnished with such accessories: they were trying to relieve every subject of the trouble, yet also of the ability, to expand his soul's forces beyond the barriers that one can set for him so as to reduce him to mere passivity and make him more pliable.

(135)

Thus the sublime does indeed – as Kant had said it would – mediate between our conceptual and our ethical capacities. Our awareness that we cannot give a conceptual account of the sublime drives us beyond the appearance of the object in search of its supersensible substrate, which is also a quest for the totality: the ultimate ground and source of the noumena. This quest is a moral good, and to obstruct it by fixating on material appearances is ethically wrong. Hence Kant's distinction between 'superstition' and 'enlightenment':

> A propensity to a passive reason ... is called *prejudice*; and the greatest prejudice of all is *superstition*, which consists in thinking of nature as not subject to rules which the understanding through its own essential law lays down as the basis of nature. Liberation from superstition is called *enlightenment*; for although liberation from prejudices generally may be called enlightenment, still superstition deserves to be called a prejudice preeminently, since the blindness that superstition creates in a person, which indeed it seems to demand as an obligation, reveals especially well the person's need to be guided by others, and hence his state of passive reason.

(161)

While many postmodern thinkers find much to admire in the Kantian notions of 'free play' and the 'abyss', this advocacy of 'enlightenment' is frequently chastised as reprehensible. It is easily presented as a will to dominate the material world by forcing it to fit our own ideas, and as equally implicated in false consciousness as the 'superstition' it seeks to eradicate. In a suggestive phrase of Kant's the enlightenment philosopher can be seen as 'raving with reason': so utterly convinced of the power and goodness of rationality as to countenance imposing its benefits on the 'superstitious' by force. Against such criticisms it might be argued that idolatry and superstition do yet greater violence to both the objective world and the subjective observer. In order to adjudicate, it will be necessary to examine the modifications to which the Kantian system was subjected by subsequent philosophers.

HEGEL AND THE DIALECTIC

Kant's *Critique of Pure Reason*, then, succeeds in establishing the existence of a transcendental subject. But this subject is placed in such a frustrating and contradictory position that some have wondered why he bothered to defend it. In all three *Critiques* we are made painfully aware that we can achieve only a perspectival understanding of our surroundings, whose true nature and purpose must always remain hidden from us. And yet the very awareness that we perceive the world from a particular point of view itself implies the possibility of a world viewed from no particular point of view. We are thus in a tragic predicament: constantly impelled to chase after an unconditioned knowledge which is by definition unattainable. In fact, as soon as we do try to lift our knowledge out of experience, we run straight into irreconcilable contradictions. Kant called these contradictions antinomies. To take one example; the concept of causality is easily proved to be true 'for us'. In any particular experience we could have, the law of cause-and-effect will pertain. However, if we depart from the realm of experience and try to apply our concept of causality to the totality of the universe, we run into an antinomy – that is, a contradiction both sides of which are equally true for us. It makes an equal amount of sense to claim that something caused the entire universe as it does to argue that the universe has no ultimate cause. In other words, antinomies arise from the attempt to apply perspectival knowledge to the totality, which is also an attempt to shift our perceptions of phenomena on to things-in-themselves. According to Kant, we can only avoid running into antinomies if we resist the temptation to fetishize our own ideas by claiming knowledge of the absolute, eternal nature of things.

This idea that the subject is unable to achieve any absolutely true knowledge can easily be interpreted as an affront to human dignity. It seems a trifle absurd, as well as unbearably tragic, that there should exist a being which is condemned ceaselessly to aspire towards this truth, while knowing that its best attempts are always already doomed to failure. It seems doubly intolerable that this unhappy being should be us. By claiming that the mind imposes its categories on the world, and that these categories produce what we can know of reality, Kant at once bestowed an unprecedented freedom on the subject and firmly limited the scope of what that subject might aspire to know. We are given our independence from material constraints at the price of eschewing any complete knowledge of our surroundings. Many subsequent thinkers took Kant's description of our predicament as a challenge; some, such as G.W.F. Hegel, seem to have taken it as a provocation.

Hegel wanted to retain the subjective freedom we glean from Kant, while eliminating the supposedly insurmountable obstacles to absolute knowledge. The thing-in-itself appeared to him as a pernicious absurdity. For what is the point of retaining as a philosophical concept something of which we can never have any knowledge? Indeed, if we can know nothing of the thing-in-itself, how can we know that it exists? What is to prevent us from claiming that the appearance of things – the reality which is posited for us by the mind – is in fact the only reality?

There are actually many reasons why such a claim is hard to sustain. In the first place, our concepts are continually changing, and there must be some reason for this. Human history shows that the most treasured beliefs of one age have very often been regarded as utter delusions by later epochs. The sheer inaccessibility of the thing-in-itself provides one explanation for this tendency of human beings to get things 'wrong'. But Hegel refused to accept this solution. Instead, he advanced the radical notion that truth is, by definition, historical:

> The bud disappears in the bursting-forth of the blossom, and one might say that the former is refuted by the latter; similarly, when the fruit appears, the blossom is shown up in its turn as a false manifestation of the plant, and the fruit now emerges as the truth of it instead.[14]

Clearly, it does not make sense to say that the appearance of the fruit means that the blossom was 'wrong'. The fruit grows out of the blossom, and could not have come into existence without it. And yet the fruit is somehow 'truer' than the blossom or, put another way, the fruit is the truth of the blossom. Hegel believes that human thought progresses in an analogous fashion. Its history forms an organic unity, in which each individual moment can only be understood in its relation to the whole. In the *Phenomenology of Spirit* (1807) Hegel gives to this whole the name *Geist*, which can be translated as either 'Mind' or 'Spirit'. This entity is closely related to earlier manifestations of the 'absolute subject', such as Descartes's 'I' and Kant's transcendental subject, but Hegel is determined that, unlike the works of the two earlier philosophers, his *Phenomenology* will leave nothing outside the scope of Spirit.

Hegel's method in this book is often referred to as 'dialectical'. Although this term goes back to Plato, Hegel gives it its characteristic modern application. The Hegelian dialectic denies the existence of self-identical entities. That is to say, Hegel assumes that nothing just is, that nothing exists 'in itself'. Rather, all identity is relational, being formed out of, or determined by its relations to other identities. This is true from a temporal perspective – for example the identity of the blossom is dependent on the bud and the fruit. It is also true from a logical perspective. For example, the notion of 'matter' can only be established by virtue of its relation to the notion of 'idea'. There is thus a sense in which the notion of 'idea' is constitutive of the notion of 'matter' – its ostensible opposite. This doctrine, which is referred to as the 'interpenetration of opposites', is of the utmost importance for future theories of false consciousness.

Hegel did not invent the notion that the opposing poles of a dichotomy define each other, and are thus constitutive of one another's identity. This idea crops up with some regularity in Western literature. When, in 'Crazy Jane Talks With the Bishop' (1932), W.B. Yeats's eponymous heroine declares that 'Fair and foul are near of kin/ And fair needs foul' (ll.7–8),[15] she echoes the prophetic revelation of Shakespeare's witches, over three centuries earlier, that 'Fair is foul, and foul is fair' (*Macbeth* I, i, 11). But Hegel was the first to schematize the theory of relational identity into a completely coherent philosophical system in which he gave it the most crucial role, making it nothing less than the motor of all human history and knowledge.

In order to become conscious of its own existence, says Hegel, the Absolute Spirit must create an opposite, an other, against which it can define itself. Since Spirit is (of course) spiritual, this other can only be material. In fact, the objective world of matter *is* this self-alienation of Spirit. Kant had discerned this situation when he understood that the transcendental subject creates the grounds of its experience out of its own a priori categories. But because his thought was 'formalist' rather than 'historicist', Kant took the inability of the subject to know the thing-in-itself as an eternal, inevitable state of affairs. As Hegel sees it, this is merely the condition which pertains while Spirit remains unaware that the material world is its own objectified form. The history of thought represents the progressive realization by Spirit of this fact. Once Spirit has achieved full self-consciousness, once it has learnt to recognize the external world as its own alienated and objectified form, the opposition between subject and object will be abolished and human history will have achieved its purpose.

The problem with Kant's notion of the unknowable thing-in-itself, according to Hegel, is that 'it takes for granted certain ideas about cognition as an instrument and as a medium, and assumes that there is a difference between ourselves and this cognition' (47). Given these assumptions of Kant's, it is possible to claim that human cognition is a faulty tool, necessarily inadequate to the thing-in-itself. If however, as Hegel believes, there is no meaningful distinction to be drawn between ourselves and our cognition, then it makes no sense to suggest that there is something of which we can know the existence but not the qualities. Our lack of knowledge of its qualities simply means that 'for us' it has no qualities, and therefore no existence. The Kantian disjunction between 'for us' and 'in-itself' thus evaporates. The 'in-itself', as Hegel puts it, 'was only an in-itself *for consciousness*' (54).

One possible conclusion which could be drawn from this would be that we do indeed perceive objects as they really are. Hegel, however, goes on to demonstrate that our sense-perceptions, far from offering transparent access to the world, actually prove to be mediated emanations from the Absolute Subject. All sense-perceptions, he remarks, depend upon the concepts 'Here' and 'Now'. But these concepts do not designate anything that exists. We say and think that we live in the 'now', in the present. But in fact, perception takes time. We do not, therefore, perceive the present, we only see the past. And the past, by definition, does not exist. Similarly, the concept 'here' is merely a formal category, which can be filled with an entirely different content simply by turning around. The ideas of 'here' and 'now', without which no sense-perception would be possible, are simply 'universal' concepts, and 'it is the universal that is the true content of sense-certainty' (60).

So the empirical road to truth is closed, because experience is produced out of universal concepts. Kant had come to a similar conclusion. But like Descartes, he had retained within the individual a transcendental ego, which could function as the ultimate guarantor of truth 'for us'. Hegel considers the option of grounding knowledge in such an individual subject:

> the vanishing of the single Now and Here that we mean is prevented by the fact that I hold them fast. 'Now' is day because I see it; 'Here' is a tree for the same reason. But in this relationship sense-certainty experiences the same dialectic acting upon itself as in the previous one. I, *this* 'I', see the tree and assert that 'Here' is a tree; but another 'I' sees the house and maintains the 'Here' is not a tree but a house instead.
>
> (61)

So the concept 'I' is also a 'universal' which is imposed upon a fluid and nebulous series of impressions. We may recall here that Hume reached much the same conclusion. But it is not Hegel's purpose to relapse into scepticism. On the contrary, he believes that by demolishing all possible grounds for immediate truth, he has established the potential for humanity to uncover the real, ultimate truth which underlies these deceiving illusions. In Hegel's thought, the characteristics of Kant's individual transcendent subject are magnified into the Absolute Subject; the universal Spirit which both creates and is the material universe, and which works through the material agency of discrete, individual human subjects.

In the *Phenomenology*, Hegel famously declares that 'the True is the whole' (11). He means that we can only make proper sense of individual ideas when we think of them in relation to the Absolute Subject. We may recall here that for Kant, this was precisely what we must *not* do. Kant had argued that when we try to reason about the totality, we come upon irreconcilable contradictions, or antinomies. Hegel retorted that in fact every concept is made up of a unity of opposite moments. To mould an abstract concept out of the flux of sensual perception, we must force these chaotic data into a determinate form, which will involve a temporary and artificial reconciliation of real conflicts. Our ideas are formed out of this 'interpenetration of opposites'. But the contradictions within the concept can be revealed by what Hegel calls a dialectical analysis. Better yet, these contradictions are resolved in the course of time, giving rise to a synthesis, which in turn contains a new contradiction, and so on.

Hegel's declaration that 'the True is the whole' thus refers us to a historical perspective. As he goes on to say, 'the whole is nothing other than the essence consummating itself through its development. Of the Absolute it must be said that it is essentially a *result*, that only in the *end* is it what it truly is' (11). What Hegel has done here is to integrate the epistemology of Kant's individual subject with the Judaeo-Christian idea of a Providential history. He revives the ancient idea that history has a meaning which is progressively revealed to those who live it. This meant, among other things, that the truth will change and develop with history. For Hegel, systematic false consciousness resulted from ignoring this fact:

> *Dogmatism* as a way of thinking, whether in ordinary knowing or in the study of philosophy, is nothing else but the opinion that the True consists in a proposition which is a fixed result, or which is immediately known.

> (23)

What Hegel's followers would soon be calling 'ideology' emerges here as a critique of abstract rationalism. It is, as Hegel puts it, 'dogmatic' to assume that human reason can attain fixed truths which will not develop and be superseded with the forward march of history. It is also 'dogmatic' to claim that a concept is 'immediate': to assert that it has an independent, or 'essential' existence, free from the influence of other concepts and from internal contradiction. Twentieth-century philosophers would refer to these two erroneous tendencies as 'ahistoricism' and 'essentialism' respectively. In Hegel, this kind of mistaken thinking produces a 'bad insight', which allows religious superstition and political repression to flourish. This does not happen automatically or by accident, but is the result of

> an evil intention by which the general mass of the people is befooled. The masses are the victims of the deception of a *priesthood* which, in its envious conceit, holds itself to be the sole possessor of insight and pursues its other selfish ends as well. At the same time it conspires with *despotism* which . . . stands above the bad insight of the multitude and the bad intentions of the priests, and yet unites both within itself.
>
> (330)

So Hegel, like most of the thinkers we have been analysing, shows how tyrannical rulers deliberately inculcate false consciousness in their subjects. In an allusion to the French Revolution, Hegel notes that 'these three aspects of the enemy' – false consciousness, priestcraft and tyranny – are under attack by the force which, following Kant, he calls 'Enlightenment'. However, Hegel's theory of the dialectical interpenetration of opposites leads him to the conclusion that Enlightenment is itself determined by the very forces it strives to overthrow:

> If all prejudice and superstition have been banished, the question arises, *What Next? What is the truth Enlightenment has propagated in their stead?* It has already declared that this positive content is in its extirpation of error. . . . In its approach to what, for faith, is absolute Spirit, it interprets any *determinateness* it discovers there as wood, stone, etc., as particular, real

things. Since in this way it grasps in general *every determinate-ness*, i.e. all content and filling, as a *human entity* and (*mere*) *idea*, absolute Being becomes for it a *vacuum* to which no determinateness, no predicates, can be attributed.

(340)

Enlightenment provides the critical tools to demolish superstition and idolatry. It follows that its own nature is defined by the prejudices it attacks, just as Rousseau's exaltation of the individual subject, reacting against the *philosophes'* degradation of the subject to the sum of its objective experiences, can be seen to be determined by the very doctrines it criticized. In Hegel, the criticism of false consciousness once again consists in the revelation that the idols of superstition are merely 'human entit[ies]'. However, since it is a merely negative, critical mode of thought, Enlightenment cannot propose alternative qualities for the Absolute which the idolaters have made anthropomorphic. As a result, Enlightenment perceives itself, quite wrongly, as completely independent of the superstition it attacks: 'it does not recognize that what it condemns in faith is directly its own thought' (344). The danger to which Hegel points here – and it is one which is amply borne out by subsequent history – is that the method we use to criticize ideology can easily turn into an ideology itself.

THE YOUNG HEGELIANS

Hegel ended his life as a respectably conservative, officially sanctioned pillar of the Prussian establishment. But the spectacularly radical potential of his ideas intoxicated a whole generation of acolytes who flourished in the Berlin of the 1840s. This group, which included the young Karl Marx and Friedrich Engels, was known as the 'Free Ones', and is now referred to as the 'Young Hegelians'. These youthful radicals – few of them were out of their twenties when they published their most important work – seized on the historicizing aspect of Hegel's thought, and developed it into a theory of political revolution.

Hegel's *Phenomenology* is at root a theology. Christianity believes in a spiritual God, who objectifies Himself in the Incarnation, and whose Providence guides human history towards an ultimate reconciliation with Himself. Hegel uses much the same narrative, but transposes it into philosophical terminology. But this in itself seemed blasphemous to many, as was revealed by the publication of David Strauss's *Life of Jesus* (1835). To the horror of the Prussian academies, Strauss announced that the Gospels were not supposed to be read as literal descriptions of historical events, but as 'mythical', or symbolic accounts of truths which were nonetheless 'real' for not being empirically accurate. Strauss's purpose was not to attack, but to defend Christianity from the mocking assaults of Voltaire and the rationalist *philosophes*:

> For as both the natural explanations of the Rationalists, and the jesting expositions of the Deists, belong to that form of opinion which, whilst it sacrifices all divine meaning in the historical record, still upholds its historical character; the mythical mode of interpretation agrees with the allegorical, in relinquishing the historical reality of the sacred narratives, in order to preserve to them an absolute inherent truth.[16]

Strauss thus attempts to establish the legitimacy of his own 'mythical' method by comparing it to ancient 'allegorical' interpretative modes. In fact, though, his work has little in common with the Patristic commentators. As he goes on to admit, 'The . . . essential distinction therefore between these two modes of explanation is, that according to the allegorical this higher [spirit] is the immediate divine agency; according to the mythical, it is the spirit of a people or a community' (26). In the Prussia of 1835, this was an astonishing confession. Strauss was claiming that the Gospels were not direct expressions of the divinity, but were mediated through the 'spirit of a people'. He was asserting, in other words, that the source of biblical inspiration was mortal.

This was the first eruption of the radicalized Hegelianism which dominates the subsequent history of philosophy. Strauss's claim was plausible because it rested on Hegel's concept of *Geist*, the universal spirit which works through human agency. The combined effect of Kant and Hegel had been to establish, through a purely rational and logical process, the existence of an Absolute Subject which determines human thought and history, and which objectifies itself in the material world. Strauss thought that the truth of Christianity could be established far more certainly through this philosophy than by relying on the dubious veracity of historical evidence. In fact, Strauss deduced the historical reality of Jesus Christ from the doctrines of Hegel:

> That which is rational is also real; the idea is not merely the moral imperative of Kant, but also an actuality. Proved to be an idea of the reason, the unity of the divine and human nature must also have an historical existence.
>
> (46)

To the Prussian clerical and academic establishment this was getting things backwards, to put it mildly, and the twenty-seven-year-old Strauss was banished forever from the academic profession. But his book had a tremendous impact. It began to dawn on people that Hegel, of late the august and austere sage of Berlin, had actually been the most dangerous iconoclast since Luther.

However, it took a critical reinterpretation of Hegel to bring out the revolutionary implications of his ideas. Just as Strauss brought the 'spiritual' source of Christianity down to earth in the 'spirit of a people', so other young Hegelians busied themselves in showing the relevance of the master's doctrines to practical affairs. In a newspaper article of 1842, Arnold Ruge announced that 'Our times are political, and our politics intend the freedom of this world. . . . This application of theory to existence is lacking in Hegel's political thought.'[17] 'Hegel's turn to theory' (230), in Ruge's view, led him to the quasi-religious conclusion that we can do nothing of our own volition to hasten the stately progress of Spirit towards self-consciousness. Ruge, on the contrary, sees no reason why Spirit's alienation should not be overcome through human agency: 'the dissolution of the abstract theoretical Spirit ... is to be brought about by involving it in political life' (256). Ruge thus proposes to abolish the age-old distinction between the material and the ideal by means of integrating Hegelian theory with political practice.

Apart from Marx and Engels, the young Hegelian whose influence was most important and long lasting was undoubtedly Ludwig Feuerbach. It has often been said that Marx turned Hegel on his head; in fact that description better fits the work of Feuerbach. Or, to put the relationship in slightly different terms, 'Feuerbach belongs to Hegel as much as the beaker of hemlock to Socrates'.[18] In *The Essence of Christianity* (1841), Feuerbach takes Strauss's revision of Hegel to its logical conclusion. He will, as he declares in the preface, carry out 'a faithful, correct translation of the Christian religion out of the Oriental language of imagery into plain speech.'[19] Like Strauss, then, Feuerbach proposes to reveal the true meaning of Christianity. Unlike Strauss, he wants to do this by using the methods of materialism: 'I do not generate the object from the thought, but the thought from the object' (xxxiv). It follows that religion is an ideal reflection which corresponds to certain causal factors in the material world:

> Religion is the dream of the human mind. But even in dreams we do not find ourselves in emptiness or in heaven, but on earth, in the realm of reality; we only see real things in the entrancing splendour of the imagination and caprice, instead of in the simple daylight of reality and necessity.
>
> (xxxix)

This is precisely the reverse of the methods of Kant and Hegel, and Feuerbach's work thus represents a radical departure in German philosophy – the turn away from idealism and towards materialism.

He refuses to locate the truth about the world in any extra-terrestrial being, whether it be God or the various philosophical substitutes which have been proposed by his precursors:

> This philosophy has for its principle, not the Substance of Spinoza, not the *ego* of Kant and Fichte, not the Absolute Identity of Schelling, not the Absolute Mind of Hegel, in short, no abstract, merely conceptual being, but a real being, the true *Ens realissimum* – man.
>
> (xxxv)

To the question of the origin of religion, Feuerbach thus gives the answer to the riddle of the Sphinx – it is man. The contention that ideology always fetishizes human qualities or activities is exemplified in the work of Feuerbach. Man is distinguished from the animals, he says, in that we are able to achieve self-consciousness, that is, to become aware that we are a species. We can clearly see the influence of Kant here. Feuerbach is saying that human beings are defined by their ability to conceptualize, to subsume the particular beneath the general. When we do this to ourselves, we come up with the concept of 'man' as 'species-being'. It is this notion of 'man' as a generalized concept that is to replace the more nebulous entities such as Descartes's ego, Kant's subject or Hegel's Spirit as the guiding principle of the world.

God according to Feuerbach, is merely an 'alienation' (today we might say a 'projection') of the infinite capacities of 'man' considered in general, as a 'species-being'. This is the truth which Christianity represents through the symbol of the Incarnation:

> And it is our task to show that the antithesis of divine and human is altogether illusory, that it is nothing else than the antithesis between the human nature in general and the human individual. . . . The divine being is nothing else than the human being.
>
> (13–14)

The history of religion, according to Feuerbach, is a continual revelation of this fact:

> Hence the historical progress of religion consists in this: that what by an earlier religion was regarded as objective, is now regarded as subjective; that is, what was formerly contemplated and worshipped as God is now perceived to be something *human*. What was at first religion becomes at a later period idolatry; man is seen to have adored his own nature. Man has given objectivity to himself, but has not recognized the object as his own nature: a later religion takes this forward step; every advance in religion is therefore a deeper self-knowledge.
>
> (13)

Feuerbach believed that he had achieved this task for religion in general, by finally demonstrating that God was merely the alienated concept of the human species. We should note here that he has simply reversed the terms used by Hegel. Where Hegel saw the objective world as the self-alienation of the Absolute Spirit, Feuerbach sees the Absolute Spirit as the self-alienation of mortal man. Because he has merely reversed Hegel, however, Feuerbach does not depart from the fundamental conceptual apparatus which he found already in place. Thus he, too, retains the notion of an Absolute Subject, only he identifies this entity with the generalized concept of humanity, its species-being. He then asserts that the material, in the form of mankind, generates and determines the ideal, in the form of God. Feuerbach, that is to say, is a materialist determinist.

We must also bear in mind that this position is quite incompatible with Hegel's dialectic. The dialectic views all binary oppositions as illusory, since they are produced and upheld by the interpenetration of opposites. It is thus undialectical to assert that one pole of the opposition (say, the material) 'determines' the other (say, the ideal), because all oppositions are mutually determining. In Hegel for example, the objectification of Spirit is a necessary pre-condition of Spirit's own self-consciousness. Feuerbach's confident claim that his work 'generates thought from the *opposite* of thought, from Matter, from existence, from the senses' (xxxv) indicates an unfortunate relapse away from the full rigour of Hegel, back towards the naive 'sensationalism' of Condillac and Destutt de Tracy. This error, which inaugurated an extremely powerful and tenacious 'materialist Hegelianism', was to prove perhaps the most costly and tragic mistake in the history of philosophy. To see why, we will have to turn to the work of Feuerbach's most perspicacious follower, Karl Marx.

4

MARXISM

Our Works are the mirror wherein the spirit first sees its
natural lineaments.

(Thomas Carlyle, *Sartor Resartus*)[1]

MARX AND MATERIALISM

Marxism has become indelibly associated with materialism. Many
Marxists have believed, and have thought that Marx himself
believed, that ideas are mechanistically determined by the material
environment. In this, Marxists recalled earlier 'metaphysical'
materialists such as Condillac and Destutt de Tracy. They allied
this materialism, however, to an emphasis on the historical process,
originally inspired by Hegel. This led them to assert that both
our objective circumstances and our subjective ideas inevitably
change and develop through history, and that this process is driven
by the material engine of the economy. The kind of economic
system under which a person lived, and the position that person
occupied within that system, were thus held to determine his or her
consciousness.

However, this interpretation of Marx is erroneous, and the

fact that it gained widespread currency is regrettable. It is based largely on *The German Ideology* (1845–6), a work composed as a polemical intervention in a topical debate, in which Marx's opponents were the idealist young Hegelians discussed in the previous chapter. To refute them, Marx makes several statements that do indeed read like materialist manifestoes. For example, announcing his departure from idealist Hegelianism, Marx declares:

> In direct contrast to German philosophy which descends from heaven to earth, here it is a matter of ascending from earth to heaven. . . . The phantoms formed in the brains of men are also, necessarily, sublimates of their material life-process. . . . Morality, religion, metaphysics, and all the rest of ideology as well as the forms of consciousness corresponding to these, thus no longer retain the semblance of independence. . . . It is not consciousness that determines life, but life that determines consciousness.[2]

Together with Marx's focus on the economy in his later work, statements such as these have misled many thinkers into a crude materialism, in which ideological phenomena are explained away by referring them to economic developments. In the Soviet Union this kind of reading was institutionalized and provided with the political power to maintain and propagate itself. There has, however, always been an alternative current within Marxism which has seen the relationship between ideas and the objective world in more sophisticated terms, and which has thus remained truer to the dialectical approach of Marx himself. For instance, in the *Theses on Feuerbach* (1845), Marx goes out of his way to criticize the reductive materialism of his predecessor:

> The chief defect of all previous materialism (that of Feuerbach included) is that things, reality, sensuousness, are conceived only in the form of the *object, or of contemplation*, but not as *sensuous human practice*, not subjectively. Hence, in contra-distinction to materialism, the *active* side was set forth abstractly

by idealism – which, of course, does not know real, sensuous activity as such. Feuerbach wants sensuous objects, really distinct from conceptual objects, but he does not conceive human activity itself as *objective* activity.

(V, 3)

Marx thus challenges Feuerbach's oppositions between subject and object, the ideal and the material. He suggests that the dichotomy between these spheres is superseded in human activity, or praxis. Since it involves the translation of mental ideas into physical effects, praxis is simultaneously material and ideal, subjective and objective. Feuerbach, like the eighteenth-century French materialists, remains trapped within a false polarity:

The materialist doctrine concerning the changing of circumstances and upbringing forgets that circumstances are changed by men and that the educator must himself be educated. This doctrine must, therefore, divide society into two parts, one of which is superior to society.

(V, 4)

It is simply a logical error, according to Marx, to reduce ideas to mere reflections of material conditions. By isolating one factor as primary or determining, Feuerbach ignores the interpenetration of opposites, and loses sight of the social totality. In the *Economic and Philosophical Manuscripts* (1844), Marx declares that 'Thinking and being are thus certainly distinct, but at the same time they are in unity with each other' (III, 299). Clearly, we could not even form the concept of an 'ideal' sphere unless we also conceived of a 'material' realm. The poles of the opposition create and define each other, and this fact is revealed in human practice, which combines thought and material activity.

Referring to his own method, Marx announces that 'consistent naturalism or humanism is distinct from both idealism and materialism, and constitutes at the same time the unifying truth of both' (III, 336). Marx intends his method to be a synthesis of idealism and materialism. The antinomy between these approaches is, in fact, definitive of false consciousness. It arises, according to Marx, because philosophers have imagined themselves as standing outside the historical process. Since history is driven by the dialectical interaction of the ideal with the material, the contradiction between these terms will be abolished once it is understood that philosophical ideas are themselves part of the material process which they describe:

> We see how subjectivity and objectivity, spirituality and materiality, activity and suffering, lose their antithetical character, and thus their existence as such antitheses only within the framework of society; we see how the resolution of the *theoretical* antithesis is *only* possible in a *practical* way, by virtue of the practical energy of man. Their resolution is therefore by no means merely a problem of understanding, but a *real* problem of life, which *philosophy* could not solve precisely because it conceived this problem as *merely* a theoretical one.
>
> (III, 302)

Here Marx applies Hegel's innovation to the theory of ideology. Previously, idealists had claimed that materialists had simply got it wrong, while materialists had found the source of illusion in idealism. But here, Marx suggests that false consciousness actually consists in the contradiction between these two schools of thought. Ideas and matter form a totality, which cannot be broken up into discrete elements without serious errors resulting. Through the unity of philosophical theory with material practice, the age-old antithesis between subject and object could be resolved, and a higher truth might therefore be achieved.

However, Marx by no means implies that this opposition is illusory. On the contrary, it is entirely real, on both a theoretical and an empirical level. The subject/object relationship really has become distorted. The polarity is thus both real and false: it is an accurate description of the wrong state of affairs. Like many of his contemporaries, Marx was aware that the independent self was entering into an antagonistic relationship with its environment, and that the progress of instrumental reason was being achieved at the expense of ethical judgement. (As Tennyson puts it in 'Locksley Hall' (1842): 'Knowledge comes, but wisdom lingers, and I linger on the shore/ And the individual withers, and the world is more and more.')[3] Since the subject/object antithesis is an accurate description of the existing situation, it can only be altered along with the situation it describes. It follows that, as Marx puts it in the *Theses on Feuerbach*, 'The question whether objective truth can be attributed by human thinking is not a question of theory but is a practical question' (III, 2). Like Hegel's progressive self-consciousness of Spirit, Marx's unity of the material and the ideal is a task to be performed, rather than a condition to be described.

Marx's most sustained analysis of the relationship between ideology and political change – *The Eighteenth Brumaire of Louis Napoleon* (1852) – does not deal in abstract theory, but studies a particular series of historical events.[4] In this text, Marx is concerned to explain how Louis, the feckless and disreputable nephew of Napoleon Bonaparte, had recently managed to bring off a *coup d'état* in France. What is striking for our purposes is the complex interplay – the dialectical interpenetration of opposites – between the influence Marx ascribes to ideas and the role he gives to material factors. He announces the complexity of this relationship right at the beginning:

> Men make their own history, but they do not make it just as they please; they do not make it under circumstances chosen by themselves, but under circumstances directly encountered, given and transmitted from the past. The tradition of all the dead generations weighs like a nightmare on the brain of the living.
>
> (XI, 103)

There is thus a mutual determination between the inherited objective circumstances in which people unavoidably find themselves, and their ability to impose their subjective will on this material environment and alter it. In Hegelian terms, Marx abolishes the opposition between the ideal and the material, by insisting that these spheres form a totality. Once again, the emphasis on the totality identifies false consciousness as the illusion that either ideas or matter is logically prior to, or causally determining of, the other. In *The Eighteenth Brumaire*, Marx turns his attention to representation, the faculty which mediates between the poles of this polarity.

Marx begins his study of Louis Napoleon with a look at the great revolutionaries of earlier eras – Luther, Cromwell, Robespierre. He points out that each of them dressed up his cause with imagery and symbols drawn from the past. In these representations they 'found the ideals and the art forms, the self-deceptions they needed to conceal from themselves the bourgeois limitations of the content of their struggles' (XI, 104). They 'needed' to deceive themselves by the use of representation, because they had to believe that their cause was absolutely righteous and true. In fact, from a later historical perspective, their struggles can be seen to have advanced the interests of nascent capitalism, and thus to have served a particular class of people in the name of all humanity. Because they were not really serving the interests of all humanity, but needed to believe that they were, they had recourse to symbols and representations to persuade themselves and others of the universality of their cause.

We can thus see that, for Marx, representation has at times exercised a determining influence on history. But this has been necessary only because the people who used it have been deluded, and have deluded others, about what they were doing. Marx warns that this is a persistent tendency:

> And as in private life one differentiates between what a man thinks and says of himself and what he really is and does, so in

> historical struggles one must still more distinguish the
> language and the imaginary aspirations of parties from their
> real organism and their real interests, their conception of them-
> selves from their reality.

> (XI, 128)

Although these 'imaginary' representations are not 'real', and in
fact conceal 'real', material interests and motives, they nevertheless
really exert a determining influence on the way people think and
behave. This is an example of how representation can actively
determine material conditions, rather than emerging out of them
as a mere 'reflection'. In fact Marx goes out of his way to point out
that, in the situation he is describing, the political representatives
of the people cannot be identified by class or economic interest.
Representation has become independent, and this autonomy
of representation is necessary to the project of falsely presenting
the particular interest of a class as if it were the general interest of
humanity:

> Only one must not form the narrow-minded opinion that the
> petty bourgeoisie, on principle, wishes to enforce an egoistic
> class interest. Rather, it believes that the *special* conditions of
> its emancipation are the *general* conditions within which alone
> modern society can be saved and the class struggle avoided.
> Just as little must one imagine that the democratic represen-
> tatives are indeed all shopkeepers[5] or enthusiastic supporters
> of shopkeepers. In their education and their individual position
> they may be as far apart from them as heaven from earth. What
> makes them representatives of the petty bourgeoisie is the fact
> that in their minds they do not get beyond the limits which the
> latter do not get beyond in life.

> (XI, 130)

To use Hegelian language again, when the particular is falsely
subsumed within the general, representation is forced to assume a

determining role which does not naturally belong to it. We recall that in Kant and Hegel, the process of conceptualization involved the subsumption of the particular intuition beneath the general concept. Here, the petty bourgeoisie has formed a false concept of itself as the universal class. Because of this concept's falsity, the normal relationship of representation to reality is distorted, and people can only see the representation, which they therefore mistake for reality. We find ourselves once more in Plato's cave.

Marx regards the delusion that representation is material and substantive as ideological. A representation is a product of the human brain, and humanity is under a constant temptation to idolize these representations, and treat them as though they were real. This temptation serves the interests of political tyranny, as in the case of Louis Napoleon, whose power depends on his ability to represent himself as his illustrious uncle. Marx is describing here the beginnings of the aestheticization of politics, which culminates in the consuming concern of postmodern politics with 'image' and 'perception'. He scornfully refers to Louis's

> expedition to Strasbourg, where a trained Swiss vulture had played the part of the Napoleonic eagle. For his irruption into Boulogne he puts some London lackeys into French uniforms. They represent the army. In his Society of December 10, he assembles 10,000 rogues who are to play the part of the people, as Nick Bottom that of the lion.
>
> (XI, 149)

Louis's power thus depends on the spurious autonomy of representation. Or rather, it depends on his ability to persuade the French people of this autonomy. He is, according to Marx, able to succeed in this only among the most ignorant and parochial elements:

> Bonaparte represents a class, and the most numerous class of French society at that, the *small-holding peasantry*. . . . Historical

> tradition gave rise to the belief of the French peasants in the
> miracle that a man named Napoleon would bring all the glory
> back to them. . . . The fixed idea of the Nephew was realized,
> because it coincided with the fixed idea of the most numerous
> class of the French people.
>
> (XI, 187–8)

Due to their ignorance and isolation, says Marx, the peasants
'cannot represent themselves, they must be represented' (XI, 187).
Most of the French people (and the French were the most highly
educated nation in the world) were unable clearly to distinguish
representation from reality. This is why they lay mired in false
consciousness, and were unable to resist, or even to desire to resit,
the *coup d'état* and despotism of Louis Napoleon.

ALIENATION AND REPRESENTATION

In the previous chapter, we saw how Kant attributed the subject's
inability to perceive the thing-in-itself to the inherent capacities of
the human mind. We also saw how Hegel historicized this obstacle
to our knowledge by describing the objective world as the self-
alienation of the Absolute Subject. Finally, Feuerbach suggests that
this Subject is nothing else than 'man' himself, in the form of an
idealist fantasy. Marx removes the last mythologizing element
from this narrative. For him, Feuerbach's identification of 'man'
with 'species-being' is simply another abstraction. Marx unites
idealism and materialism through his recognition that the essence
of 'man' which has become alienated is no abstraction, but is
actually nothing more mysterious than our own activity, our
labour.

Feuerbach had argued that the being we call 'God' is actually
only a projection of the capacities of the human species. When we
worship 'God', therefore, we really adore an alienated form of ourselves. Marx concurs, remarking of 'men' that 'The products of
their brains have got out of their hands. They, the creators, have

bowed down before their creations' (V, 23). The religious strictures against idolatry again loom large here. For Marx, however, this alienated form of human activity is incarnated in the material products of our labour: 'The product of labor is labor which has been embodied in an object, which has become material: it is the objectification of labor' (III, 272). This, rather than Feuerbach's abstract 'species-being', is the true objectification of mankind's essence.

Under a capitalist economy, however, this objectified essence of our selves does not even belong to us. The product made by the worker belongs to the capitalist, who considers it as a commodity to be sold. This leads Marx to emphasize that capitalism involves an alienation of our selves, as well as an objectification. What is more, under the system of wage-labour the worker's own labour-power becomes a commodity, which he or she sells for money. Money thus represents human labour in objectified form. As such it functions as the 'universal commodity', against which everything can be measured, which can be exchanged for anything, and which makes universal exchange possible. When we alienate our activity (which is to say our lives, our selves) in the form of commodities, and then allow these commodities, in the abstract shapes of finance and the market, to dictate and command our lives, we therefore commit a secular form of idolatry. We fetishize 'the works of men's hands', and allow alienated human activity to exert a determining influence over human life. Our objectified labour dominates our subjective labour. As Marx puts it in *On the Jewish Question* (1843), 'Money is the estranged essence of man's work and man's existence, and this alien essence dominates him and he worships it' (III, 172).

The fact that money represents human labour, that it is human labour in objectified form, had already been noted by the Scottish economist Adam Smith. In the *Economic and Philosophical Manuscripts*, Marx points out that Smith has thus repeated once again the critical response to all kinds of superstition since Luther;

he has unmasked it as the fetishization of human activity, which transforms the subject into an object:

> To this enlightened political economy, which has discovered – within private property – the *subjective essence* of wealth, the adherents of the monetary and mercantile system, who look upon private property only as *an objective* substance confronting men, seem therefore to be *fetishists, Catholics. Engels* was therefore right to call *Adam Smith* the *Luther of Political Economy.*
>
> (III, 290)

Once again, the false consciousness of earlier economists had been the result of a mistaken attitude to representation. Money is originally merely a symbol, which mediates between various objects, acting as a common denominator so as to facilitate exchange. However, when we sell our own lives for money, we lose sight of its merely symbolic role. As Marx says in *Comments on James Mill* (1844):

> It is clear that this *mediator* thus becomes a *real God*, for the mediator is the *real power* over what it mediates to me. Its cult becomes an end in itself. Objects separated from this mediator have lost their value. Hence the objects only have value insofar as they *represent* the mediator, whereas originally it seemed that the mediator had value only insofar as it represented *them.*
>
> (III, 212)

The problem of false consciousness, then, is for Marx a problem of representation. Ideology consists in an inability to recognize the mediating function of representation, in assuming that it is an autonomous sphere, and thus mistaking the appearance for the thing-in-itself. Marx's thought is clearly Kantian here. But Marx mingles this influence with the Hegelian view that identity is relational and historical. Ideology also involves a blindness to the fact that our concepts are mediated through their relations to other concepts. Describing the process of 'ideological subdivision', Marx observes that 'In consciousness – in jurisprudence, politics, etc. – relations become concepts; since they do not go beyond these relations, the concepts of the relations also become fixed concepts in their mind' (V, 92).

We have thus identified three main elements in Marx's notion of ideology: the idolatry of human activity, the mistaking of the sign for the thing, and the conversion of 'relations' into 'fixed concepts'. Thus far, he seems quite 'idealist'. However, Marx's aim was to transcend the opposition between idealism and materialism, which he saw as itself a symptom of false consciousness. In accordance with this purpose, he connects these ideal errors with a particular kind of economic system. In order to investigate the nature of this connection, we must turn to Marx's most detailed criticism of ideology: *Capital* (1867).

Marx founds this work on a minute analysis of the commodity, which he undertakes in the first chapter.[6] Following Aristotle, he points out that an object can be regarded in two ways: as something to be used (in which case one is concerned with its 'use-value') and as something to be exchanged (in which case one thinks of its 'exchange-value'). If two objects with different use-values (say a desk and a chair) are to be exchanged, some way must be found to render them equivalent. We must find a way to say 'x desks = y chairs'. In fact, for the purposes of exchange, we must be able to perceive the ideal value of the desk in the material object which is the chair. But since the desk is not materially the same as the chair, this equivalence can only be figurative. We must, that is, impose an alien and ideal representation, or 'form of value', on the material objects. We therefore no longer see the thing-in-itself, we see only the 'commodity form' – our own idea or concept – which we have imposed upon it.

As with Hegel's adaptation of the idea that opposites are mutually definitive, Marx's notion of the 'form of value' involves a newly systematic application of a venerable intuition. As we have seen, the knowledge that exchange-value and use-value imply two completely different ways of conceiving objects goes back to Aristotle, and it recurs frequently in literary history. Thus Thomas Traherne, in his autobiographical reflections from the 1660s, recalls how, as a child, he gradually learned to recognize the symbolic value of commodities:

> It was a difficult matter to persuade me that the tinselled ware upon a hobby horse was a fine thing. They did impose upon me and obtrude their gifts that made me believe a ribbon or a feather curious. I could not see where was the curiousness or the fineness: And to teach me that a purse of gold was of any value seemed impossible, the art by which it becomes so, and the reasons for which it is accounted so, were so deep and hidden to my inexperience. . . . [but as he grew older] The glass of imagination was the only mirror, wherein anything was represented or appeared to me. . . . So I began among my play-fellows to prize a drum, a fine coat, a penny, a gilded book &c . . . who before never dreamed of any such wealth. . . . So that the strange riches of man's invention quite overcame the riches of Nature, being learned more laboriously and in the second place.[7]

So, rather than discovering the concept of exchange-value, Marx simply relocates it within an over-arching philosophical tradition. Specifically, Marx uses the notion of exchange-value as an explanation for our inability, noted by Kant, to perceive the thing-in-itself. As a result of 'the fetishism of the commodity', we no longer see the 'real' thing, but only its 'form of appearance'. In keeping with his Hegelian background, however, Marx also offers us a way out of this frustrating situation. Just as, for Hegel, alienation would be transcended when Spirit recognized matter as its own alienated self, so for Marx alienation will be abolished when human beings understand that the 'market forces' which shape their lives are nothing but representations of their own alienated activity.

We may note here that there is a sense in which Marx's solution to the central problem of philosophy is 'materialist': he connects it to the economy. On the other hand, the capitalist economy is itself made possible by a gigantic and purely ideal delusion. There is no material difference between a rose regarded as an object of beauty, and a rose regarded as a commodity for sale. The difference – which is none the less real for not being material – exists only in the mind of the beholder. Like the spurious symbols used by Louis Napoleon, the commodity form is a representation which falsely assumes a material appearance, and thereby comes to exert a pernicious determining influence on material circumstances. It is, in other words, a purely ideological phenomenon.

Marx illustrates the ideological effects of exchange-value with a quotation from Shakespeare's *Timon of Athens*:

> What is here?
> Gold? Yellow, glittering, precious gold!
> No, gods, I am no idle votarist:
> . . . Thus much of this will make
> Black white, foul fair, wrong right,
> Base noble, old young, coward valiant.
> . . . This yellow slave
> Will knit and break religions, bless th'accursed,
> Make the hoar leprosy adored, place thieves
> And give them title, knee, and approbation
> With senators on the bench.
>
> (IV, iii, 25–38)[8]

In his commentary on this speech, Marx points out that to see something as a commodity is to view it as what it is not; to perceive the ideal representation of some other thing within the material body of the object. Money, the generalized commodity-form, spreads this illusory perception throughout society, dissolving all previous identities and distinctions, and remoulding human consciousness in its own image. In the fully developed form of capital, money achieves an active, self-generating power through which it shapes the lives of concrete individuals. It is therefore, says Marx, a 'visible god' (III, 324). Timon also perceives in the gold an invitation to idolatry; he refuses to worship it as an 'idle votarist'. For Shakespeare as for Marx, the material medium of representation known as money at once expresses, embodies and produces an idolatrous consciousness.

In the twentieth century the alien significance which exchange-value imposes upon the thing-in-itself has often been explored through the concept of humanity's alienation from the world of objects. In Jean-Paul Sartre's *Nausea* (1938) for instance, the protagonist Roquetin is afflicted by a feeling that material things have become possessed with an unnatural and nauseating active power:

> Objects should not touch because they are not alive. You use them, put them back in place, you live among them: they are useful, nothing more. But they touch me, it is unbearable. I am afraid of being in contact with them as though they were living beasts.[9]

How do objects achieve this power of subjective agency? Marx's theory suggests that they are the repositories of fetishized human activity. Georg Simmel's *The Philosophy of Money* (1900) reaches a similar conclusion by a quite different route. Simmel argues that the value we attach to an object cannot, by definition, be objective. Nothing is valuable in itself; the value of an object is created by the subject's desire for it. Just as for Kant the human mind creates the objects of its experience, so for Simmel it is subjective desire which creates the value of those objects. But this does not mean that value is purely subjective, either. If it was not incarnated in an object, value could have no existence. In fact, value mediates between subject and object. It is 'a third category, which cannot be derived from either subject or object, but which stands, so to speak, between us and the objects.'[10] Value is representation; it is created when we represent our subjective desire in a material object.

In order to exchange one object for another, however, we must conceive of them as equivalent in value. This means that we need a common denominator in which the values of the two objects can be expressed. This common denominator is thus the objectified form of value, as Simmel points out, 'The value of an object becomes objectified by exchanging it for another object' (81). Value thus takes on an existence which is independent of the objects being exchanged, and this objectified value is represented in the form of money:

> Money is the representative of abstract value. . . . All other
> objects have a specific content from which they derive their
> value. Money derives its content from its value; it is value
> turned into a substance, the value of things without the things
> themselves.
>
> (120–1)

Money is thus the material representation of abstract value. It is the 'third term', the 'mediator' between subject and object, which has been given a purely objective form. It is clear, then, that Simmel agrees with Marx that money involves an objectification of subjective activity – it occludes the subjective element in the creation of value, rendering value completely objective. It thus also involves a distortion of the relationship between ideas, matter and representation, conflating the third term of this trinity with the second. To the extent to which this objectified mediator dominates social life – the degree to which we live in a 'money economy' – we might therefore expect that all forms of representation would come to seem autonomous and aspire to exert a determining influence over human life. This is one way of characterizing the ideology of the 'postmodern condition'. However, for the first half of the twentieth century Marxists generally conceived of ideology in materialist fashion, as empty ideas whose true determination could be found in the material world. How did this misinterpretation of Marx gain such widespread currency?

THE MATERIALIST FALLACY

As we have seen, the relationship in Marx's work between the ideal, the material and the representational is extremely complex, and it would be a gross simplification to claim that false consciousness is 'caused' by one of these factors alone. Unfortunately, the most immediately influential of Marx's followers, his friend and collaborator Friedrich Engels, sometimes commits precisely this error. At times, Engels seems to agree with Marx that false consciousness consists in rigid, 'metaphysical' antitheses, such as the one between ideas and matter. Thus, in the *Anti-Duhring* (1877–8), he gives the following description of false consciousness, or 'metaphysics':

> To the metaphysician, things and their mental reflexes, ideas, are isolated, are to be considered one after the other and apart from each other, are objects of investigation fixed, rigid, given once and for all. He thinks in absolutely irreconcilable antitheses. . . . For him a thing either exists or does not exist; a thing cannot at the same time be itself and something else. Positive and negative absolutely exclude one another; cause and effect stand in a rigid antithesis one to the other.
>
> (XXV, 22)

The 'metaphysician', in other words, commits the two cardinal sins against Hegel: ahistoricism and essentialism. He sees things as eternal, self-identical essences, and he remains unaware of either the historical process by which they come into being, or of their mediation and determination by other things. This account of ideology corresponds to the tendency Marx identifies in *Capital*, by which we impose an alienated, fetishistic image upon an object, thus obscuring the labour which produced it and its relation to other objects. However, Engels does not apply these strictures to his own 'scientific' methodology, which consequently comes to seem rather 'metaphysical' itself. For example, Engels constructs just such a 'rigid antithesis' between materialism and idealism. He claims that 'Marx and I were pretty well the only people to rescue conscious dialectics from German idealist philosophy and apply it in the materialist conception of nature and history' (XXV, 11). This was necessary, he says, because 'Hegel was an idealist. . . . This way of thinking turned everything upside down, and competely reversed the actual connection of things in the world' (XXV, 25). Engels has evidently forgotten here about the inter-penetration of opposites, and the mutual definition of the poles of dichotomies. As a result, he lapses into the most brutal kind of materialist determinism. Due to his and Marx's efforts,

> it was seen that *all* past history was the history of class struggles; that these warring classes of society are always the products of the modes of production and of exchange – in a word, of the *economic* conditions of their time; that the economic structure of society always furnishes the real basis, starting from which we can alone work out the ultimate expla-nation of the whole superstructure of juridical and political institutions as well as of the religious, philosophical, and other ideas of a given historical period. But now idealism was driven from its last refuge, the philosophy of history; now a material-istic treatment of history was propounded, and a method found of explaining man's 'knowing' by his 'being', instead of, as heretofore, his 'being' by his 'knowing'.
>
> (XXV, 26–7)

The unequivocal absolutism of Engels's opposition, together with his assertion that a particular relation of cause-and-effect always remains constant in human history, is about as far away from Marx's historical dialectics as it is possible to be. The whole tenor

of Marx's *oeuvre* suggests that to claim that one side of an opposition necessarily determines the other is itself an ideological error,
which can be traced to a particular historical configuration of ideal
and material forces.

Engels makes this mistake in the *Anti-Duhring*. However, the
proposition that the economic structure of society always determines every idea anyone ever has is difficult to defend for long,
and Engels was forced to retreat somewhat from this position. In a
letter to Bloch, composed in 1890, Engels writes:

> According to the materialist conception of history the deter-
> mining element in history is *ultimately* the production and
> reproduction of real life. More than this neither Marx nor I have
> ever asserted. . . . The economic system is the basis, but . . .
> the reflexes of all these actual struggles in the brains of the
> combatants: political, legal, philosophical theories, religious
> ideas and their further developments into systems of dogma –
> also exercise their influence upon the course of the historical
> struggles and in many cases may preponderate in determining
> their *form*.[11]

We should notice here that Engels is backing off only from
the empirical claim that the economy is *always* the *only* determining factor. He still does not recognize the theoretical objection
that, according to the dialectics of Hegel and Marx, it is logically
impossible to separate the material sphere from the ideal.
Consequently, he is left in the position of asserting that the
economy merely determines people's ideas quite a lot, and quite
often. The difference is only one of degree, and the contradiction
with his own dialectical method remains intact. As we shall see, this
is an error which crops up with disturbing regularity in the history
of Marxist thought.

Ironically enough, one of the first alarms about the dangers
of economic determinism was sounded by George Plekhanov,
the Russian Marxist who was to become the major theoretical

influence on Lenin, and thus on the ultra-materialist theory which came to dominate institutional Communism in the twentieth century. In *The Materialist Conception of History* (1897), Plekhanov differentiates between 'economic materialists' and 'dialectical materialists'.[12] The former group, he says, remain trapped within the 'theory of factors'. That is, they do not think of society as a 'totality', but instead try to isolate a 'factor' (in this case the economy) and claim for it a determining influence. As Plekhanov points out, this way of thinking is precisely what Hegel and Marx criticized: 'A historico-social factor is an abstraction, and the idea of it originates as the result of a process of abstraction' (15–16). That is to say, economic determinism 'dismembers the activity of social man and converts its various aspects and manifestations into separate forces, which are supposed to determine the historical movement of society' (17).

Tragically for the subsequent history of institutional Marxism, Plekhanov's thought is not so clear when he comes to discuss the method of the so-called 'dialectical materialists'. Plekhanov claims that, instead of identifying abstract 'factors', this approach takes a 'synthetic' view of society, viewing it in its 'totality' (18). But when he begins to describe exactly what this involves, Plekhanov can only talk of 'explaining the activity of social man by his needs and by the means and methods of satisfying them prevailing at the given time' (20). Incisive and pertinent when identifying the errors of the 'economists', Plekhanov is hard-pressed to suggest a significantly different, alternative kind of 'materialism'. In fact, his most cogent statement of his own opinion only avoids relapsing into a 'theory of factors' by reducing all 'social relations' to the level of material 'productive forces':

> The history of ideologies is to a large extent to be explained by the rise, modification and breakdown of associations of ideas under the influence of the rise, modification and breakdown of definite combinations of social forces ... men do not make

> several distinct histories – the history of law, the history of
> morals, the history of philosophy, etc. – but only one history,
> the history of their own social relations, which are determined
> by the state of the productive forces in each particular period.
> What is known as ideologies is nothing but a multiform reflec-
> tion in the minds of men of this single and indivisible history.
>
> (44)

Plekhanov's work is thus materialist, not only in the sense that
he believes the ideal is *caused by* the material, but also in that he
believes that the ideal actually *is* material. Human ideas are simultaneously 'reflections' of productive forces and a part of the 'one
history' of material 'social relations'. This view would become
extremely influential in the twentieth century, when thinkers such
as Gramsci and Althusser sought for alternatives to the causal,
determinist materialism espoused by Plekhanov's most famous
disciple, V.I. Lenin.

In *Materialism and Empirio-Criticism* (1908) Lenin does his
utmost to enlist Marxism under Plekhanov's banner of 'dialectical
materialism', which he quite wrongly claims was Marx's own term
for his ideas. In the course of this effort he forgets that his mentor's
approach emphasized the dialectical, rather than the materialist,
element of this phrase. Lenin therefore abandons Plekhanov's
concept of the totality, and lapses definitively back into a 'theory
of factors'. The 'empirio-criticism' of the book's title refers to
a theory recently advanced by one of Lenin's political rivals,
Bogdanov. Using recent discoveries in physics, which suggested
that atoms were not solid matter but were made up of relations
between electrons, Bogdanov had proposed that there was no
intrinsic difference between physical and mental phenomena.
Rather, these were merely different ways of organizing the same
experiences. Appalled at what seemed to him an infernal mixture
of Berkelean idealism and Humean scepticism, Lenin vehemently
defended two main propositions: that there is a material world

which exists outside the subject, and that this world causes the mental activity of that subject:

> All knowledge comes from experience, from sensation, from perception. That is true. But the question arises, does *objective reality* 'belong to perception,' i.e., is it the source of perception? If you answer yes, you are a materialist. If you answer no, you are inconsistent, and will inevitably arrive at subjectivism.[13]

Lenin thus insists on the most rigid opposition between the ideal and the material. Although his later work evinces some softening of his position, here he propagandizes furiously in favour of materialist causality, and perceives only deception and turpitude in idealist 'subjectivism'.

The centralized organization of the Bolshevik party, the repressive methods to which the party found itself impelled after the revolution, and the rise to power after Lenin's death of the theoretically unsophisticated Josef Stalin, all contributed to the establishment of this naively reductive materialism as the official philosophy of the Marxist world. This was a tragedy in two senses. Most importantly, it gave a crude plausibility to the megalomaniacal ambitions of such 'engineers of the soul' as Stalin and Mao. But more relevantly for our purposes here, it reintroduced the use of the term 'ideology' in the Napoleonic sense: as designating vague, nebulous ideas which claim independence from material circumstances. The resulting confusion has plagued the theory of ideology ever since.

THE RETREAT FROM MOSCOW: GEORG LUKÁCS

The first theorist to make a significant advance on Marx's theory of ideology while remaining true to the dialectical approach of Marx himself was the Hungarian Communist leader, theoretician and literary critic, Georg Lukács. His *History and Class-consciousness* (1922) bases its entire theory on the first chapter of *Capital,* which Lukács says 'contains within itself the whole of historical materialism'.[14] At first glance, this seems a rather surprising claim because, as we have seen, *Capital*'s first chapter is concerned with the fetishism of the commodity – that is to say, with an ideological, rather than a material problem. And yet Lukács's book does succeed in convincingly demonstrating that commodity fetishism is the central, definitive characteristic of capitalist society.

We should recall here that in *Capital*'s first chapter, entitled 'The Commodity', Marx shows how exchange-value emerges out of the relationship between two commodities by means of a process of figuration, so that, for instance, when a coat is exchanged for a piece of linen,

> The linen expresses its value in the coat; the coat serves as the material in which that value is expressed . . . the physical body of commodity B becomes a mirror for the value of commodity A.

> (Marx, 139, 144)

Commodity exchange presupposes the real presence of the value of one object in the physical body of another. This value is not, of course, materially present, but it is nevertheless actually present. Thus commodity exchange depends on the ability of a figure, a symbol, to become real. It depends, that is to say, on the power of ideas to impose themselves on material reality – the Kantian 'appearance' must supersede the 'thing-in-itself'. This is achieved by introducing a common denominator, which will express the value of materially distinct objects as though they were the same. The medium through which this illusory equivalence is achieved is human labour: not any particular act of labour, but human labour considered in general, in the abstract form for which the universally recognized symbol is money. But to objectify and abstract human labour (that is to say, human activity, human life itself) demands a specific kind of false consciousness. Lukács will term this ideological phenomenon reification, which means 'to turn into a thing'. In *Capital*, Marx describes its effects as follows:

> the commodity-form ... is nothing but the definite social relation between men themselves which assumes here, for them, the fantastic form of a relation between things. In order, therefore, to find an analogy we must take flight into the misty realm of religion. There the products of the human brain appear as autonomous figures endowed with a life of their own, which enter into relations both with each other and with the human race. So it is in the world of commodities with the products of men's hands. I call this the fetishism which attaches itself to the products of labor as soon as they are produced as commodities, and is therefore inseparable from the production of commodities.
>
> (Marx, 165)

Lukács's achievement is to show how this commodity fetishism, and its concomitant 'reified consciousness', have permeated every aspect of capitalist society. He insists, repeatedly, on the total nature of this phenomenon – 'Reification requires that society should learn to satisfy all its needs in terms of commodity exchange' (91); 'the basic structure of reification can be found in all the social forms of modern capitalism' (171); 'Reification is, then, the necessary; immediate reality of every person living in capitalist society' (197). This ubiquitous and evil tendency freezes relations and processes, so that they appear as immutable, self-identical 'things'. It erases mediation and history, making the actually fluid phenomena of society appear as 'supra-historical essences' (14). It obscures the fact that identity is relational, and thus makes it hard to consider society as a 'totality'. In the form of the 'market', it transforms relations between people into relations between the products of their labour. In short, reification is the tendency to fetishize our own activity, when that tendency has grown into a universal and determining influence over every aspect of our lives.

In this description of a thoroughgoing false consciousness, Lukács has recourse to the Aristotelian concept of 'second nature'. As we have seen, Aristotle's notion referred to 'custom': when we have done things a certain way for a long time, we assume this is the 'natural' way to do them. Lukács gives this concept a more materialist inflection. The commodity is a product of human labour. For it to be possible 'for the commodity structure to penetrate society in all its aspects and to remold it in its own image' (85), we must endow these products with an autonomous existence. 'Men', says Lukács, 'erect around themselves in the reality they have created and "made", a kind of second nature which evolves with exactly the same inexorable necessity as was the case earlier on with irrational forces of nature' (128). Once again, false consciousness consists in allowing this 'second nature', which is only 'the works of men's hands', to exert a fetishistic dominance over our lives.

Lukács regards the philosophical tendency to separate the ideal from the material as another result of reification. Because the workers must sell their labour-power as a commodity (they must objectify their own activity), the duality between subject and object enters into the subject itself. Just as, for Hegel, Spirit alienates itself in the material world, so in Lukács the human subject objectifies its own activity. This gives rise to what Lukács calls 'reflection theories', which try to reduce one pole of the subject/object dichotomy to a mere 'reflection' of the other:

> In the theory of 'reflection' we find the theoretical embodiment of the duality of thought and existence, consciousness and reality, that is so intractable to the reified consciousness. And from *that point of view* it is immaterial whether things are to be regarded as reflections of concepts or whether concepts are reflections of things. In both cases the duality is firmly established.
>
> (200)

It follows that materialism is merely an 'inverted Platonism' (202), a 'mythology' which is produced by the reification of what is actually a *relation* into two separate *things*. On a theoretical plane, then, the way out of false consciousness demands that '*things should be shown to be aspects of processes*' (179), because 'the *developing tendencies of history constitute a higher reality than the empirical "facts"*' (181).

This is why Lukács declares, in a statement which is in direct contradiction to Leninist orthodoxy, that 'It is not the primacy of economic motives in historical explanation that constitutes the decisive difference between Marxism and bourgeois thought, but the point of view of the totality' (27). Earlier modes of thought had reached the same conclusion, as Lukács admits,

> God, the soul, etc. . . . are nothing but mythological expressions to denote the unified subject or, alternatively, the unified object of the totality of the objects of knowledge considered as perfect (and wholly known).
>
> (115)

However, this totality had previously been doomed to remain a philosophical abstraction, since there had not existed any material means to realize it in the real world. Lukács believes Marx discovered this practical instrument in 'the standpoint of the Proletariat'. The 'proletariat' was another word for the 'working classes'. It referred to people whose income was derived from selling their labour-power for wages. (It is important to note that, by this definition, almost everyone today is a 'proletarian', and that Marx's theories are thus not rendered obsolete by the recent numerical decline of the industrial working classes.) When Marx and Lukács wrote, however, there were many other social classes in Europe: a landowning aristocracy, a smallholding peasantry, and a capitalist or 'bourgeois' class which owned the factories and mines in which the proletarians worked. Of these, only the proletariat was able to achieve consciousness of the process of reification. It was able to do this because, by selling their labour-power, its members objectified themselves, turning themselves into commodities. In Hegel, history works towards an end, or *telos*, in which Spirit recognizes the material world as its own alienated condition. In Marx and Lukács, history functions so as to reveal to the proletariat that capital, the force which dominates and controls their lives, is nothing more than their own objectified labour. This knowledge of the interpenetration of object and subject is what Lukács means by the proletariat's 'class-consciousness'.

As a result of this revelation, there will no longer be a need for an ideological false consciousness. The antinomies between subject and object, ideas and matter, will therefore dissolve, and the totality will become visible. For the moment, then, philosophy's task is to show the proletarians that the reified, fragmentary and contradictory world in which they live is simply the product of their own objectified activity: 'to deduce the unity – which is not given – of this disintegrating creation and to prove that it is the product of a creating subject. In the final analysis, then: to create the subject of the "creator"' (140). The problems which plagued Kant and Hegel will then evaporate, as Lukács rhapsodically anticipates 'The genesis, the creation of the creator of knowledge, the dissolution of the irrationality of the thing-in-itself, the resurrection of man from his grave' (141).

Using a similar line of reasoning, Engels had once declared that 'the German proletariat is the heir of classical German philosophy'. We can, perhaps, imagine the reaction of a German proletarian on being informed of this illustrious lineage. Marxism as a whole takes a large gamble when it bestows the task of reconciling all philosophical contradictions on a group of fallible and very busy human beings. In its materialist manifestations, Marxism has assumed that the proletarian revolution is an inevitable event. Since material circumstances determine ideas, the theory runs, it will be possible to deduce the point at which the workers will rebel simply by analysing the progress of the economy. However, a dialectical view of the relations between ideology and material activity cannot share this confidence. Lukács chooses to end *History and Class-consciousness* on a pessimistic note:

> History is at its least automatic when it is the consciousness of the proletariat that is at issue. The truth that the old intuitive, mechanistic materialism could not grasp turns out to be doubly true for the proletariat, namely that it can be transformed and liberated only by its own actions, and that the 'educator must himself be educated'. The objective economic evolution could do no more than create the position of the proletariat in the production process. It was this position that determined its point of view. But the objective evolution could only give the proletariat the opportunity and the necessity to change society. Any transformation can only come about as the product of the – free – action of the proletariat itself.
>
> (208–9)

So it is perfectly possible that the proletariat will choose not to take this action. Once capitalism has achieved a certain level of prosperity for practically all of its denizens, the charms of the commodity may come to seem preferable to the arduous and dangerous quest for revolution. The fact that one's consciousness is reified, that one sees only appearances and representations rather than the things-in-themselves, may come to seem rather unimportant. As we know, this is what did in fact occur. There were no successful proletarian revolutions in western Europe, and the proletariat settled down in front of the television to enjoy its commodified world in peace. The task of philosophy from this point on is the 'negation' – the criticism – of this virtually universal false consciousness.

HEGEMONIC STRUCTURES: ANTONIO GRAMSCI

Antonio Gramsci's *Prison Notebooks* (written 1929–34) represent the first theoretical attempt to come to terms with the defeat of the proletarian revolution. Following the failure of the Italian workers to seize power in the years following the First World War, Gramsci, the leader of the Italian Communist Party, was imprisoned by Mussolini's Fascist government. Ironically enough, this confinement gave him a unique freedom to re-evaluate many of the doctrines which Moscow forcibly imposed on politically active Communists. Like Lukács, Gramsci jettisoned any kind of materialist determinism. Given his situation, it was obvious that there was nothing inevitable about the triumph of the proletariat. The revolution had failed, despite the fact that the 'objective', material conditions for its success had been in place. Gramsci therefore sought for the reasons for his defeat in the subjective, ideological, control which the capitalist state exercised over its inhabitants.

Gramsci's view of ideology is best approached through two passages from Marx, to which he returns repeatedly in the *Prison Notebooks*. Discussing the question of revolutions, Marx writes:

> In considering such transformations a distinction should always be made between the material transformation of the economic conditions of production, which can be determined with the precision of natural science, and the legal, political, religious, aesthetic or philosophic – in short, ideological forms in which men become conscious of this conflict and fight it out.[15]

Gramsci glosses this passage as saying that 'men acquire consciousness of structural conflicts on the level of ideologies' (365), and goes on to maintain that it 'should be considered as an affirmation of epistemological and not simply psychological and moral value' (164). That is to say, Gramsci believes that revolutions, while they may be facilitated by shifts in the economic structure, are also fought out, and their outcomes are decided, on the level of 'ideologies'. Consequently, he devotes an enormous amount of attention to conflicts between different systems of ideas. The other major source for Gramsci's conception of the relationship between ideology and political power is Marx and Engels's *Communist Manifesto* (1848), where it is announced that 'the ruling ideas of each age have ever been the ideas of its ruling class' (VI, 503). This is the so-called 'dominant ideology thesis', which suggests that the class which is economically dominant will try to impose its own peculiar way of seeing the world on society as a whole. The realm of ideology thus becomes a field of class conflict, and it is this battle which Gramsci sets out to study using the concept of hegemony.

By this term, Gramsci means the nexus of material *and* ideological instruments through which the ruling class maintains its power. Hegemony is thus a form of praxis. This allows Gramsci to reserve the term 'ideology' for pure consciousness, and he proposes to 'distinguish between historically organic ideologies, those, that is, which are necessary to a given structure, and ideologies that are arbitrary, rationalistic, or 'willed' (376–7). The former may be specific to a particular class, or 'group', but they are an accurate expression of that group's material interests. Interestingly, Gramsci identifies the latter kind of ideology with the mechanistic mode of thought exemplified by Destutt de Tracy's 'science' of 'Idéologie'. Because it traces the formation of ideas to material sensations, this kind of approach is, in Gramsci's view, utterly mistaken. He claims that Marxism

> represents a distinct advance and historically is precisely in opposition to Ideology. Indeed the meaning which the term 'ideology' has assumed in Marxist philosophy implicitly contains a negative value judgment and excludes the possibility that for its founders [i.e. Marx and Engels] the origin of ideas should be sought for in sensations, and therefore, in the last analysis, in physiology.
>
> (376)

The theory that ideologies are merely pale reflections of material influences is, according to Gramsci, unable to account for the existence of 'organic' ideologies, which are necessary and in a sense true. Materialism wrongly presupposes an essential distinction between matter and ideas. The result of this tendency in Destutt, and also in Marxist 'economistic superstition' (164), has been a three-fold error:

1 ideology is defined as distinct from the structure, and it is asserted that it is not ideology that changes the structures but vice versa;

2 it is asserted that a given political situation is 'ideological' – i.e. that it is not sufficient to change the structure, although it thinks that it can do so; it is asserted that it is useless, stupid, etc.;

3 one then passes to the assertion that every ideology is 'pure' appearance, useless, stupid, etc.

(376)

So Gramsci reacts against the notion of ideology as false consciousness, asserting that 'all systems have an historical validity, and are necessary' (138). This also involves a reaction against the belief that ideology is a mere reflection of material circumstances. The effect of these advances is to thrust an immense importance on to the sphere of ideas. In fact, Gramsci points out that material factors are only ever expressed and understood through consciousness, and that developments in the history of consciousness can thus be more significant than economic changes:

It may be ruled out that immediate economic crises of themselves produce fundamental historical events; they can simply create a terrain more favourable to the dissemination of certain modes of thought.

(184)

Because '"popular beliefs" and similar ideas are themselves material forces' (165), any revolutionary theory must deal with class conflict on the level of ideas at least as much as in the economic arena. In fact, Gramsci is unwilling to distinguish between these two levels, preferring his notion of 'hegemony', which constitutes a '"historical bloc", i.e. unity between nature and spirit (structure and superstructure), unity of opposites and of distincts' (137).

Gramsci thus pointedly declines the metaphor, drawn from Marx but popularized by Engels and Lenin, of the economic 'base' on which is founded an ideological 'superstructure'. For him, the material sphere is itself a 'structure', which may be allied with and analogous to, but does not 'support', a 'superstructure' of ideas. These ideas, Gramsci notes, are institutionalized in 'civil society': the law courts, the bureaucracy, the religious and educational systems, and the mass media. In western Europe (as opposed to Russia) these 'ideological' institutions are more important in upholding the hegemony of the ruling class than any 'purely' economic factors:

> The superstructures of civil society are like the trench-systems of modern warfare. . . . In Russia the State was everything, civil society was primordial and gelatinous; in the West there was a proper relation between State and civil society, and when the State trembled, a sturdy structure of civil society was at once revealed.
>
> (235, 238)

Thus we can see how Gramsci's theory of hegemony could explain the failure of the revolution in western Europe. Although the years following the First World War produced unprecedented economic crises, which rocked states like Germany and Italy to their foundations, people's ideas remained in thrall to the ruling powers. The pressing need, as Gramsci saw it, was to determine how this had been possible, and this would entail a careful analysis of the institutions which transmitted ideology to the people. From his prison cell, Gramsci was able to do no more than suggest where such a study might begin:

The school as a positive educative function, and the courts as a repressive and negative educative function, are the most important State activities in this sense: but, in reality, a multitude of other so-called private initiatives and activities tend to the same end – initiatives and activities which form the apparatus of the political and cultural hegemony of the ruling classes.

(258)

Because Gramsci's view of the relative autonomy of ideology was in such direct contrast to the official position of the rest of the European Communist leadership, these suggestive insights were not followed up for over thirty years. They do, however, form the major inspiration behind the work of Louis Althusser, which in turn became the most significant influence on post-war debates about ideology.

5

POST-MARXISM

There can't be any doubt about it any longer: the struggle against ideology has become a new ideology.

(Bertolt Brecht)[1]

ALTHUSSER AND MATERIALISM

The work of Louis Althusser espouses a materialism which is deeply collusive with the process of objectification it purports to criticize. It is thus significant that Althusser's ideas, often filtered through the works of his pupil Michel Foucault, have become the decisive influence on postmodern critiques of ideology. In particular, the anti-Hegelian aspects of Althusser's thought – his emphasis on the materiality of ideas, his opposition to 'totalizing' systems of thought, his attack on the subject – have won an appreciative audience, and spawned a vogue for vulgar materialism which is only now beginning to subside.

In *Lenin and Philosophy* (1971), Althusser explores Gramsci's burgeoning but unfulfilled interest in the material institutions which administer ideology to the masses. This book's most influential chapter, 'Ideology and Ideological State Apparatuses', pursues Gramsci's reference to capitalism's 'need to elaborate a new type of man suited to the new type of work and productive process' (Gramsci, 286). The first task of any economic system, according to Althusser, is to reproduce its own conditions of production. This involves reproducing the kinds of people who will be able to participate in the process of production. The power of the modern capitalist state to do this is dependent on two types of institutions: the 'Repressive State Apparatuses', such as the police, law courts and army, and the 'Ideological State Apparatuses', which include the Church, the family, political parties, media and – most important – the education system. As we might expect, the difference between the 'RSAs' and the 'ISAs' is that 'the Repressive State Apparatus functions "by violence", whereas the Ideological State Apparatuses function "by ideology".'[2]

'Ideology' is therefore embodied in material practice. Althusser notes that 'an ideology always exists in an apparatus, and its practice, or practices. This existence is material' (166). We saw in the last chapter that Gramsci had said much the same. But Althusser claims it follows from this that 'Ideas have disappeared as such' (168). Althusser thus reaches the peculiar and unwarranted conclusion that, due to the fact that ideas are expressed and trans-mitted by material institutions, ideas are themselves material. To assert otherwise, he claims, is 'ideology':

> the ideal and spiritual existence of 'ideas' arises exclusively in an ideology of the 'idea' and of ideology, and let me add, in an ideology of what seems to have 'founded' this conception since the emergence of the sciences, i.e. what the practices of the sciences represent to themselves in their spontaneous ideology as 'ideas', true or false. Of course, presented in affirmative form, this thesis is unproven. I simply ask that the reader be favorably disposed towards it, say, in the name of materialism. A long series of arguments would be necessary to prove it.
>
> (165–6)

It would indeed require a long series of arguments to prove that ideas are material. The fact that Althusser asks his readers to accept this as a matter of faith should be a signal that we have returned to a species of that 'metaphysical' materialism which typified the French Enlightenment. The polemical commitment to materialism which characterizes his work enables Althusser to slide from the presupposition that matter determines ideas into an assumption that ideas do not exist:

> the existence of the ideas of his belief is material in that *his ideas are his material actions inserted into material practices governed by material rituals which are themselves defined by the material ideological apparatus from which derive the ideas of that subject.*
>
> (169)

If ideas are material then the subject which has ideas must, in fact, be an object. The very notion of an autonomous subject, like the concept of non-material ideas, is said to be ideological:

> the category of the 'subject' is constitutive of ideology, which only exists by constituting concrete subjects as subjects. . . . The existence of ideology and the hailing or interpellation of individuals as subjects are one and the same thing.
>
> (173, 175)

Here we have the origin of the objectified subject celebrated by the postmodernists. Ideology, says Althusser, exists before the individual. When the concrete individual comes along, ideology has 'always already' determined a specific set of roles, a particular subjectivity, into which the individual will be slotted. This occurs through a process of 'interpellation', which basically means that a person will be systematically addressed, or 'hailed', in such a way as to force him or her into this pre-allocated 'subject-position'. Nor is this process unique to twentieth-century capitalism, for 'the formal structure of all ideology is always the same' (177). Ideology is not a historical phenomenon, but is rather an inherent tendency within the human mind which, it seems, cannot bear very much reality. The paradigmatic example of an ideological 'structure' is Christianity, which, as Althusser sees it, interpellates its followers as individual subjects by 'reflecting' such an image back to them through the Absolute Subject, who is God:

> We observe that the structure of all ideology, interpellating individuals as subjects in the name of a Unique and Absolute Subject is *speculary*, i.e. a mirror-structure, and *doubly* speculary: this mirror duplication is constitutive of ideology and ensures its functioning. Which means that all ideology is *centred*, that the Absolute Subject occupies the unique place of the Centre, and interpellates around it the infinity of individuals into subjects in a double mirror-connexion such that it *subjects* the subjects to the Subject, while giving them in the Subject in which each subject can contemplate its own image (present and future) the *guarantee* that this really concerns them.
>
> (180)

It is interesting to note that Althusser actually concurs with Christianity, and with post-Christian philosophers such as Hegel, that individuals are derived from the Absolute Subject. However, because Althusser assumes that anything which is not material is not real, he presupposes that such a Creator must produce purely illusory creatures. Or rather, since he cannot deny that the individual subject does apparently enjoy a real existence, he emphasizes the 'artificial' nature of the creative process, and insinuates that there is something repressive and underhand about it.

In Althusser's defence, it should be noted that the objectified subjects he describes do correspond to Marx's and Lukács's diagnoses of capitalism's dehumanizing effects. But whereas Marx and Lukács lament this loss of unified subjectivity as the most horrible of capitalism's evils, Althusser blithely accepts it as the correct and inevitable state of affairs. It remains for him only to scratch his head at the befuddlement of previous millennia and to deride their idealist mythologies. The fact that Althusser's theories remain extremely influential testifies to the extent to which reification has penetrated the minds of even capitalism's declared adversaries.

Any attempt to identify ideology with material practice is Quixotic because the ideal/material opposition is a mutually defining dichotomy; that is to say, the very notions of 'ideal' and 'material' would be meaningless without each other. It is one thing to argue that this polarity is at root illusory and pernicious: Hegel and Marx both thought so, and they suggested ways in which it might be possible to transcend it, and thus overcome alienation. But Althusser does not do this; rather he simply collapses one pole of the opposition into the other, and announces that ideas have 'disappeared'. He means by this that ideas do not exist 'in the mind'. Instead, they only exist in material practice, in which case, of course, they are not ideal but material. Althusser misses the point that just because ideas are manifested in praxis (which is precisely the unity of ideas and concrete activity), they are not therefore reducible to it. What is more, if there are no ideas there can be no subject to 'have' ideas. Althusser claims that the subject is itself formed by and composed of material practice, in which case it is not logically a subject at all: it is an object. Once again, a mutually defining opposition has been reduced to one of its terms. In order to sustain this reductionism, Althusser is forced to take up some original positions, which have come to form the basis of many postmodern theoretical assumptions.

As a loyal member of the French Communist Party, Althusser was concerned to establish that his materialism accorded with Marx's own teachings, and this is the task he undertook in his radically innovative *For Marx* (1969). As we saw in the last chapter, many of Marx's texts are explicitly opposed to materialism. To circumvent this fact, Althusser argues that there are actually *two* Marxes, separated by a yawning methodological chasm: 'This "epistemological break" divides Marx's thought into two long essential periods: the "ideological" period before, and the scientific period after, the break in 1845.'[3] This 'break', then, occurs with the composition of *The German Ideology* – that is, with the only one of Marx's texts which is susceptible to a consistently materialist interpretation.

For Althusser, 'ideology' is the imaginary way in which people experience their real lives, the ideal representation of a material process. Despite his sometimes tortuous formulations of the term, it is not too crude to say that Althusser ultimately equates ideology with 'idealism', by which he means the tendency to attribute a real existence to purely ideal phenomena, and to the subject in particular. 'Science', which Althusser calls the 'knowledge of' ideology, is generally used as an approximate term for a 'materialism' whose task it is to explain the source of these ideas, and so reveal their role in maintaining the power of the capitalist class, or 'bourgeoisie'. Althusser lays heavy stress on this opposition, warning of the need to preserve 'science' from 'the threats and taints of idealism, that is, of the *ideologies* which besiege it' (170), and calling for 'a continuous struggle against ideology itself, that is, against idealism' (ibid.).

By this definition, Hegel is clearly an 'ideological' thinker, and even the proto-materialist Feuerbach still relies on the non-material concept of 'species-being', thus falling prey to 'an idealist *anthropology*' (89). The early Marx succumbs to a similar 'humanism' when he makes alienated labour his central concern. This is because Marx perceives alienation as the objectification of human life, and thus as a negation of the human subject. For Althusser, of course, there is no human essence which is not always already material, and thus no subject which could be alienated by being made into an object. As a result, he must conclude that 'in Marxism, *negativity* and *alienation* are *ideological* concepts that can only designate their own *ideological* content' (214–15).

Althusser is determined to rid Marx of all traces of idealism. The major problem with this is the looming presence of Hegel throughout Marx's work. If one reads Marx as a materialist, this troublesome Hegelian heritage can be disposed of by a simple inversion, which transfers its metaphysical baggage into the material realm:

> Hegel explains the material life, the concrete history of all peoples by a dialectic of consciousness (the people's consciousness of itself: its ideology). For Marx, on the other hand, the material life of men explains their history; their consciousness, their ideologies are then merely the phenomena of their material life. This opposition certainly unites all the appearances of an 'inversion'.

(107)

A further problem arises here, however. In Hegel, one seminal contradiction – the objectification of Spirit – produces all the others. What is more, the founding unity which is Spirit is also the ultimate destination and purpose – the 'end' – of history. This is why Hegel's thought is frequently called totalizing and teleological. Now, if one were to argue that Marx had simply 'inverted' Hegel, turning the ideal elements of his system into material equivalents, one would need to find a material substitute for this founding unity of Spirit. But the real world and the process of material history appear on a purely empirical level to be so complex and discontinuous that no such original force can be identified. Thus, says Althusser, 'Marxism . . . rejects the theoretical presupposition of the Hegelian model: the presupposition of an original simple unity. . . . This presupposition has not been "inverted", it has been eliminated' (198).

Althusser's determination to read Marx as a materialist thus leads him to reject the notion that Marx founds his theory on a single, original contradiction. For example, the neo-Hegelian concept of alienated labour cannot be the basis of Marxism for Althusser, since it partakes of 'the ideological myth of a philosophy of origins' (ibid.). Since Marxism is a 'science' and Hegelianism an 'ideology', and since 'a science is not obtained by inverting an ideology' (192), Marx must be made to depart from the position that the problems of the world can ultimately be traced to one all-encompassing contradiction. Here Althusser is forced to read strenuously against the grain. There is, in fact, one fundamental contradiction which runs through all of Marx's work: the opposition between labour and capital or, as it is expressed in the early works, between human activity and the alienated form of human activity. As Lukács shows, this single opposition informs and determines every aspect of life under capitalism, moulding people's consciousness as well as dictating their economic activity. But the notion of alienation is too 'ideological' for Althusser to tolerate. He thus dismisses 'the Hegelian model and its faith in the resolving "power" of the abstract contradiction as such: in particular, the "beautiful" contradiction between Capital and Labour' (104), and so he is led inexorably to the conclusion that 'the apparently simple contradiction is always overdetermined' (106).

This use of the term 'overdetermination' is Althusser's major contribution to the theory of ideology. It means that every situation has more than one determining factor. For example, the specific form taken by oppression in twentieth-century France cannot be reduced to merely economic factors. At a glance, one can see that other, ideal forces such as conceptions of race or gender, are at work. Althusser is thus willing to concede a 'relative autonomy of the superstructures' (111). The ideas we have about the world, in other words, are not only produced by our material lives, but also attain a certain degree of independence, and can come to play a partially determining role in history. This line of reasoning is often portrayed as Althusser's departure from crude materialism. But, as we have seen, he is forced to elaborate the concept of overdetermination precisely as a result of his own ultra-materialist determinism. To reiterate: Althusser wants to eliminate all traces of Hegelian idealism, or 'ideology', from Marx. This means that he refuses to accept the validity of Marx's notion of alienated labour, which merely 'inverts' Hegel's description of alienated Spirit. He thus cannot read Marx as employing the Hegelian notion of a single, informing contradiction: the material world is visibly more complex than that. He is therefore driven, despite himself, to allow ideas to have a certain determining influence on the material world.

However, this conclusion is diametrically opposed to Althusser's materialist agenda. There are two possible ways out of this contradiction. As we saw in our discussion of *Lenin and Philosophy*, one solution, albeit a very paradoxical one, is simply to declare that ideas are in fact material. In *For Marx*, Althusser stresses instead the '*determination in the last instance by the (economic) mode of production*' (111). Although ideas may attain a 'relative autonomy', and so appear, in certain circumstances, to be independent of the material base, we are asked to retain our faith that the economy is actually the hidden, ultimate cause of ideological phenomena. As he readily admits, Althusser derives this notion from Engels's letter to Bloch, which we discussed in Chapter 4. Like that letter, it amounts to little more than a ritualistic declaration of faith in a debased and diluted materialism, which is given no empirical or logical justification.

Althusser's influence on contemporary thought has been as profound as it has been malign. In particular, as a result of Althusser's emphasis on the constitutive role of ideology, significant doubt has been cast on the concept of 'false consciousness'. All forms of idealism, he argues, are ideological. And yet it is impossible to imagine a society which did not think to some degree in idealist terms (due to the fact, which Althusser does not recognize, that the ideal and the material define each other). It follows that 'ideology is not an aberration or a contingent excrescence of History: it is a structure essential to the historical life of societies' (232). This is, surely, to stretch the term 'ideology' until it is emptied of significant content. But there is yet a further problem with Althusser's model. If 'ideology' is an illusory consciousness, and if 'science' is the 'truth of' ideology, how – given the inevitability of ideology – does one make the transition from one to the other? Here we come upon what is perhaps Althusser's most enduring legacy to postmodernism: the central role played in his theory by the aesthetic dimension.

A MATERIALIST AESTHETIC?

The problem of art is a particularly thorny one for any theory which is concerned to identify and account for false consciousness. Aesthetic statements cannot accurately be called false, but neither do they make any claim to be true. As Sir Philip Sidney pointed out in *The Defence of Poesy* (1595), 'for the poet, he nothing affirms, and therefore never lieth'.[4] In Chapter 3 we saw how Kant uses the category of aesthetic judgment to mediate between his epistemology and his ethics – that is, between his theory and its practical effects. Art performs a similar function in Althusser's work. In *Lenin and Philosophy* he declares

> *I do not rank real art among the ideologies*, although art does have a quite particular and specific relationship with ideology. . . . What art makes us *see*, and therefore gives to us in the form of '*seeing*', '*perceiving*' and '*feeling*' (which is not the form of *knowing*), is the *ideology* from which it is born, in which it bathes, from which it detaches itself as art, and to which it alludes.
>
> (221–2)

It seems that 'art' (which term remains suspiciously undefined) occupies an area midway between 'science' and 'ideology'. It also seems as though art provides a conduit by which one may pass from ideology to the 'knowledge' which is science. It does this by unmasking the contradictions within ideology, making them visible by imposing upon it a predetermined aesthetic form. This is the argument pursued by Althusser's friend Pierre Macherey, in

A Theory of Literary Production (1966). Macherey begins from the proposition that 'literary' language is essentially different from other modes of expression. It 'does not concern itself with distinctions between the true and the false, in so far as it establishes . . . its own truth'.[5] Literature takes up a position in between truth and falsehood; it twists and distorts 'the everyday language which is the language of ideology' (59), thus distancing the reader from this language, drawing attention to its ideological nature, and so making possible a later transition to a scientific 'knowledge' of ideology:

> We could offer a provisional definition of literature as being characterized by this power of parody. Mingling the real uses of language in an endless confrontation, it concludes by *revealing* their truth. Experimenting with language rather than inventing it, the literary work is both the analogy of a knowledge and a caricature of customary ideology.
>
> (ibid.)

Because literary language must mould ideology into a form dictated by pre-existent literary convention, the astute critic will be able to perceive the contradictions in ideology within the literary text. According to the Althusserian framework, these contradictions will not be visible in everyday life, where ideology is successfully able to smooth them over:

> there can be no ideological contradiction, except if we put ideology into contradiction with itself. . . . By definition, ideology can sustain a contradictory debate, for ideology exists precisely in order to efface all trace of contradiction. Thus, an ideology, as such, breaks down only in the face of the real questions. . . . Ideology's essential weakness is that it can never recognize for itself its own real limits: at best it can learn of these limits from elsewhere, in the action of a radical criticism.
>
> (130–1)

These limits, so the argument runs, are made visible when ideology is forced into a form not of its choosing, as when it must conform to the generic requirements of a particular literary mode. They can be exposed through a twofold method of analysis. As critics, we must first study the 'conditions of possibility' of the aesthetic work. These are to be sought outside the text, in the historical circumstances which produced it. Second, we must examine 'the conditions of those conditions' – the ideology which upheld and legitimated the historical situation – and these can be discerned within the text itself. Thus, in the example Macherey gives, the late works of Tolstoy emerged out of the dilemma felt by liberal Russian intellectuals between the revolutions of 1905 and 1917. This situation, in which the necessity of revolution was recognized but its feasibility was denied, gave rise to a resigned pacifism which acknowledged the existence of oppression but precluded any resistance to it. This, according to Macherey, is the ideology which Tolstoy expresses, and it is possible to discern the limitations of this ideology through a close reading of his books.

There are many difficulties with Macherey's book, not the least of which is the lack of an adequate definition of 'literature'. Macherey attempts to remedy this in a later essay, 'On Literature as Ideological Form', co-authored with Etienne Balibar. Nowhere are the limitations of the Althusserian approach to ideology more clearly displayed. The authors are scrupulously materialist, declaring that 'The objective existence of literature is . . . insepar-able from given social practices in given ISAs.'[6] This means that literature must be studied in the context of the education system, and particularly in the light of the French division of schools into 'primary-technical' institutions for training the working classes, and a 'secondary-advanced' level which produces the bourgeoisie. In the first kind of school only basic language skills are taught, in the second these are augmented with the ability to manipulate language stylistically, in 'literary' ways. Macherey and Balibar claim that, since literary texts contain both these kinds of language,

'*Literary language is itself formed by the effects of an ideological class contradiction*' (51). However, literary works subordinate the straightforward, denotative language of the workers to the ornate, connotative mode of the bourgeoisie: this is in fact the definitive characteristic of literature. It follows that 'The effect of domination realized by literary production presupposes the presence of the dominated ideology within the dominant ideology itself' (58), and thus that for the proletariat, 'reading is nothing but the confirmation of their inferiority . . . domination and repression by literary discourse of a discourse deemed "inarticulate," "faulty" and inadequate for the expression of complex ideas and feelings' (57).

This is the bleak but logical conclusion of Althusserian materialism, which does not conceive of representation or ideas other than as they are embodied in material practices. A more sophisticated consideration of literature's relationship to ideology can be found in the controversy over German Expressionism which took place during the 1930s. Expressionism was an avant-garde school of poetry, music and the visual arts, roughly comparable to surrealism in France, or to modernism in Britain. It aimed to produce a shock-effect by presenting a discontinuous, jarring and fractured view of the world. A good example of the kind of technique labelled 'Expressionist' is the cinematic device of montage, in which meaning is conveyed through the rapid juxtaposition of apparently unconnected images. In English literature, expressionistic techniques were pioneered by writers such as T.S. Eliot, in poems such as 'The Waste Land' (1921):

'On Margate Sands.
I can connect
Nothing with nothing.
The broken fingernails of dirty hands.
My people humble people who expect
Nothing.'

      la la

> To Carthage then I came
>
> Burning burning burning burning
> O Lord Thou pluckest me out
> O Lord Thou pluckest
>
> burning
>
> (ll.300–11)[7]

The form as well as the content of works like this was supposed to reflect the fragmentary and disconnected experience of life in capitalist modernity. In the 1930s, the ideological implications of this kind of art became the subject of a heated debate among European Marxist intellectuals. Georg Lukács, as might be expected from the Hegelian author of *History and Class-consciousness*, attacked Expressionism on the grounds that its fragmentary style obscured society's true interconnections, which actually formed a 'totality'. In response, Ernst Bloch noted that the subjective experience of capitalism's commodified world was itself confused and fragmentary, and suggested that Expressionism might be an accurate reflection of the way things are: 'What if authentic reality is also discontinuous?'[8] Lukács, in turn, readily conceded that the world *seems* chaotic and disordered. But he argued that this is an ideological illusion, which conceals the underlying unity of the coherent totality:

> Bloch's mistake lies merely in the fact that he identifies this state of mind directly and unreservedly with reality itself. He equates the highly distorted image created in this state of mind with the thing itself, instead of objectively unravelling the essence, the origins and mediations of the distortion by comparing it with reality.[9]

In Lukács's view, modernist writers like Joyce or Beckett limit themselves to evoking the ideological appearance of life under capitalism, whereas realist authors such as Balzac or Thomas Mann penetrate beneath this fragmentary surface to illustrate the real, though hidden, unity of social relations.

It is thus clear that Lukács has given the totality a 'metaphysical' status. He is ready to admit that no one experiences the capitalist world as a totality. But this does not mean that it is not, in fact, a totality – it just means that false consciousness has become universal. As Lukács's opponents were quick to point out, however, there is a sense in which a universal consciousness is real, if not necessarily true. The reification which Lukács himself diagnosed in *History and Class-consciousness* cannot simply be ignored or dismissed as an illusion. Rather, as Theodor Adorno stresses, it must be accepted as the actual, objective condition of the world. When a work of art expresses this reified consciousness through devices of distortion and discontinuity, it is therefore more 'realistic' than the traditional, coherent, unifying 'realism' which Lukács finds in Balzac and Mann. According to Adorno, avant-garde art faithfully reflects the subjective consequences of reification, and thus offers an ironic, critical perspective on the commodified world:

> In the form of an image the object is absorbed into the subject instead of following the bidding of the alienated world and persisting obdurately in a state of reification. The contradiction between the object reconciled in the subject, i.e. spontaneously absorbed in the subject, and the actual unreconciled object in the outside world, confers on the work of art a vantage-point from which it can criticize actuality. Art is the negative knowledge of the actual world.[10]

The most realistic modes of art, then, are those whose forms exhibit most clearly the reified condition of reality, which reproduces itself within the subject. As Adorno puts it elsewhere, 'The fetish character of the commodity is not a fact of consciousness; rather . . . it produces consciousness.'[11] This idea, first expressed by Lukács, that the commodification of the external world is paralleled in every aspect of internal, mental activity, forms the basis of the account of ideology offered by the group of thinkers known as the Frankfurt School.

THE FRANKFURT SCHOOL

The philosophers associated with the Institute for Social Research (which was originally based in Frankfurt, Germany) accomplished the most profound insights into the impact of the commodity on consciousness. The group's best-known members – Theodor Adorno, Max Horkheimer and Herbert Marcuse – based their investigations on the analysis of commodification given by Marx, in *Capital*'s opening chapter; and on Lukács's development of Marx's description into a comprehensive theory of reification. As Horkheimer notes in 'On the Problem of Truth' (1935), for Marxism 'every thesis necessarily follows from the first postulate, the concept of free exchange of commodities . . . knowledge of all social processes in the economic, political and all other cultural fields will be mediated by that initial cognition.'[12] As we have seen, Marx argues that the process of exchange involves the mental imposition of a false, ideal, equivalence on objects which are actually, materially, different. In a society in which exchange is the dominant form of economic organization – in a 'market economy' – the principle of exchange comes to dominate people's consciousnesses. A false appearance obscures the thing-in-itself, as objects are regarded for their exchange-value rather than for their intrinsic uses, and representation consequently becomes autonomous. This process affects intellectual as well as economic life. As Horkheimer puts it, explaining the rise of nominalism in 'The End of Reason' (1941):

> The objects could be regarded as an unqualified mass in philosophy because economic reality had levelled them, rendering all things equivalent to money as the common denominator. In the face of such levelling, the proper being of the object is no longer taken into account.[13]

The problem, we should note, is not to do with the 'objective', material conditions of production, to which materialist Marxists refer, but with a distortion of the subject:

> The methods for the production of social wealth are available, the conditions for the production of useful natural effects are largely known, and the human will can bring them about. But this spirit and this will themselves exist in false and distorted form.
>
> (412)

Commodity fetishism involves the idolization of subjective human activity, so that the products of that activity, 'even though summoned up by men themselves, face them as incalculable forces of destiny' (ibid.). Once again, false consciousness consists in idolizing 'the works of men's hands'. In a diabolical irony, these products then re-enter the subject in a distorted and distorting form which issues in 'the displacement of feelings into exchange-value'.[14] The process of objectification is not confined to the workplace, but becomes a habit of mind, so that people conceive of themselves and of others as objects. Worse still, the completely commodified world does not permit one to opt out of this process. This allows Adorno to characterize liberal Western democracy as 'totalitarian': 'When the feelings seize on exchange-value. . . . It corresponds to the behavior of the prisoner who loves his cell because he has been left nothing else to love' (280).

The potential effects of this fetishism were forcefully impressed upon the members of the Institute when, as refugees from the Nazis, they arrived in the USA. The culture shock which these patrician, central-European, Marxist intellectuals experienced on finding themselves in southern California was profound and productive in equal measure. They evidently found that their new environment provided ample confirmation of the philosophical theories they had absorbed in Germany. Adorno and Horkheimer's *Dialectic of Enlightenment* (1944) contains their most comprehensive account of the American experience. It is remarkable for its sustained tone of horrified fascination with the sheer power of the commodity. The potency of this force led them to the worrying conclusion that we are entering a new, surreal mode of consciousness in which 'Real life is becoming indistinguishable from the movies'.[15]

It does not surprise Adorno and Horkheimer that 'the impotence and pliability of the masses grow with the quantitative increase in commodities allowed them' (xiv–xv), that 'public opinion has reached a state in which thought inevitably becomes a commodity, and language the means of promoting that commodity' (xi–xii), or that 'the economic apparatus . . . equips commodities with the values which decide human behavior' (28). But what really shocks and disturbs them is the distorting effect of the representations imposed by commodification on the intellect: 'Representation is exchanged for the fungible – universal interchangeability. . . . The identity of everything with everything else is paid for in that nothing may at the same time be identical with itself' (10–12). The intrinsic identity of things, their use-value, is occluded when they are viewed as abstract, symbolic exchange-value. This 'levelling domination of abstraction' (11) dulls the critical faculties, ensuring that 'ideology expends itself in the idolization of given existence and of the power which controls technology' (xvi).

These two aspects of ideology – instinctive deferral to 'the facts' as they are immediately represented to us, and blind faith in instrumental science – are the most dangerous effects of commodity fetishism. In order for a thing to become a commodity, the coercive power of human reason must be exerted over the thing-in-itself: we must represent it as what it is not, and then take the representation for the reality. But this power of reason is purely formal, because it must be universally applicable without regard to the concrete materiality – the content – of the things it considers. It thus ultimately issues in the fetishization of abstract reason itself: 'Before, the fetishes were subject to the law of equivalence. Now equivalence itself has become a fetish' (17). The result is that the formal, abstract principles of reason, as manifested in the natural sciences, are held to be the only means to objective truth. In the words of Horkheimer, 'The tattered veil of money has given way to the veil of technology.'[16]

Having been fetishized as uniquely capable of producing true insight, the methods of the natural sciences are erroneously applied to the sphere of the human sciences, with disastrous results. Empirical facts are taken as 'given', that is, they are assumed to be automatically significant, without any mediation. This Hegelian term alludes to the fact that everything that exists 'for us' is made possible by its relation to other things – nothing is self-identical. In order, therefore, to understand a brute fact, we must interpret it in the light of the other facts which give it significance by providing its context. In Hegelian terms, facts are only meaningful when they are mediated through the totality.

Perhaps some examples may be useful here. Today, in the USA, statistics show that a disproportionate amount of crime is committed by young black men. This is a 'fact'. Taken in isolation, this fact might well be interpreted as indicating that young black men are predatory and dangerous people, in need of supervision and restraint. This is what Adorno and Horkheimer would regard as 'ideological' thinking. But if this fact is mediated through the totality, if it is interpreted in the context of slavery and segregation, policing tactics and media representation, the education and welfare systems, then one might well read this 'fact' as leading to the opposite conclusion: that young black men are oppressed and victimized people, in need of assistance and opportunity. At another level, in the realm of intellectual endeavour, the fetishization of 'pure' facts gives rise to the privileging of natural science, and its indiscriminate application without regard for social consequences. The most conspicuous results of this process, for Adorno and Horkheimer, were the gas chambers and the atomic bomb. The commodification of consciousness, then, produces a way of seeing the world which is not merely false but actually evil:

> That the hygienic shop-floor and everything that goes with it, the Volkswagen or the sportsdrome, leads to an insensitive liquidation of metaphysics, would be irrelevant; but that in the social whole they themselves become a metaphysics, an ideological curtain behind which the real evil is concentrated, is not irrelevant.[17]

There is, running through *Dialectic of Enlightenment* a disturbing analogy – sometimes overt, more often implicit – between the open dictatorship of Nazi Germany and the subtle totalitarianism of commodity-bound California. The formally free American society compels a conformism which constrains every aspect of life, and which is the more insidious for being experienced as voluntary:

> But freedom to choose an ideology . . . everywhere proves to be freedom to choose what is always the same. The way in which a girl accepts and keeps the obligatory date, the inflection on the telephone or in the most intimate situation, the choice of words in conversation, and the whole inner life . . . bear witness to man's attempt to make himself a proficient apparatus, similar (even in emotions) to the model served up by the culture industry. The most intimate reactions of human beings have been so thoroughly reified that the idea of anything specific to themselves now persists only as an utterly abstract notion: personality scarcely signifies anything more than shining white teeth and freedom from body odor and emotions. The triumph of advertising in the culture industry is that consumers feel compelled to buy and use its products even though they see through them.

(167)

Herbert Marcuse reached a similar conclusion in *One-dimensional Man* (1964):

> The means of mass transportation and communication, the commodities of lodging, food and clothing, the irresistible output of the entertainment and information industry carry with them prescribed attitudes and habits, certain intellectual and emotional reactions which bind the consumers more or less pleasantly to the producers and, through the latter, to the whole. The products indoctrinate and manipulate; they promote a false consciousness which is immune against its falsehood.[18]

This, according to the Frankfurt School, is the essence of commodity culture. Consciousness recognizes itself as false but it does not care, because a true consciousness would be either practically unattainable, intrinsically impossible, or – and here we reach the territory of postmodernism – actually undesirable.

ENLIGHTENMENT AND THE IDEOLOGY OF THE PRIMITIVE

The process of 'enlightenment', which enables us to recognize ideology, thus seems to be a rather mixed blessing. As Hegel noted, the same reason which allowed Voltaire to expose religious 'infamy' can itself become a fetishistic object of superstitious veneration. What is more, the rationality of the Enlightenment has, in practice, furnished a pretext for all kinds of domination and exploitation: the rule of the commodity over humanity, the hegemony of mankind over the natural world, the intellectual triumph of instrumental science and empiricist philosophy, the assumed superiority of the present over the past, and the rule of the European possessors of reason over the 'primitive' inhabitants of the 'undeveloped' world. An uneasy sense that enlightened reason is somehow complicit with the 'primitive' superstition against which it battles is expressed in numerous literary texts of the early twentieth century. In Joseph Conrad's *Heart of Darkness* (1902), for example, Kurtz – the European ivory-trader who writes reports for 'the International Society for the Suppression of Savage Customs' – is himself seen to 'regress' to a 'barbaric' condition as soon as he is removed from the artificial restraints of 'civilization'.

A strikingly perspicacious study of the arrogance of Western reason is provided by Max Weber, in *The Protestant Ethic and the Spirit of Capitalism* (1904). This work raises the question of why Protestant societies are particularly proficient at developing and exploiting a capitalist economy, which Weber defines as resting 'on the expectation of profit by the utilization of opportunities for exchange'.[19] Rather than stressing the impact of commodification on consciousness, however, Weber is interested in the more general process of 'rationalization' which is necessary for the imposition of formal equivalence on objects, but which is also manifested in new ways of organizing human behaviour. In a capitalist society, the working of the labour-force and the morality of private life must be brought into line with the method of rational calculation on which an exchange-based economy depends. As Weber puts it, capitalism demands that all aspects of society must be made to correspond to 'the natural sciences based on mathematics and exact and rational experiment' (24).

Weber shows how Protestantism, and in particular the Calvinist concept of predestination, provided a system of ideas which encouraged and legitimated the growth of a capitalist economy. According to Calvin, the salvation or damnation of each human soul had already been decided before the creation of the world. It followed that nothing one might do in one's life could possibly affect one's status in the eyes of God. In a Christian society, the effect of this doctrine would be to lay a heavy burden of anxiety on believers, who would naturally be curious about the nature of their eternal dwelling place. This concern could be allayed by searching one's life for evidence of God's favour, and this evidence seemed to be strikingly provided by material prosperity. There was thus, according to Weber, an intense psychological imperative on the

Calvinist faithful to amass as much wealth as possible in their earthly lives, and this is the source of the 'Protestant work ethic'.

Weber notes that this 'spirit' of capitalism is frequently present before any glimmer of actual capitalist activity. Clearly, then, he rejects the materialist premise that a particular economic system produces a corresponding ideology. But, as he emphasizes, 'it is, of course, not my aim to substitute for a one-sided materialistic an equally one-sided spiritualistic causal interpretation of culture and of history' (183). Like Lukács and Adorno, Weber observes analogous developments in the realms of ideology and the economy, but he refuses to reduce one to the other. However, the real challenge of Weber's book is its implication that Enlightenment rationality is not intrinsically a truer or better way of thinking than those followed by historically or geographically distant societies. This kind of relativism was profoundly shocking in the Europe of 1904. It indicated that noble systems of thought could be used to justify the most base impulses. It also raised the question of whether any system of thought could be judged superior to another. If the great process begun by Protestantism and completed by the Enlightenment – the elimination of irrational superstition from the thought of the European intelligentsia – was simply a mask for some basically shabby economic motives, then how could the professors of Paris and Berlin feel superior to the natives of the Congo or of the Dakota territories? What, in other words, gave Europeans the right to rule the rest of the world?

Sigmund Freud's *Totem and Taboo* (1913) provides an interesting answer to this question, as well as a committed defence of enlightened reason. Like Althusser, Freud attacks idealism in the name of a materialism which is no less dogmatic and reductive than the beliefs it criticizes. In an earlier work, *Three Essays on the Theory of Sexuality* (1905), Freud noted, with regard to the fetishistic displacements he observes in the sexual development of children, 'Such substitutions are with some justice likened to the fetishes in which savages believe that their gods are embodied.'[20]

He assumes that human societies progress in a manner comparable to the maturation of an individual, so that 'primitives' are essentially child-like. This belief leads him, in *Totem and Taboo*, to discount the 'savages' own accounts of why they invest particular objects with supernatural powers. The 'primitives' say that these objects are inhabited by demons. Freud refuses this explanation on Feuerbachian grounds:

> It would be another matter if demons really existed. But we know that, like gods, they are the creations of the human mind: they were made by something and out of something.[21]

Freud thus begins from the assumption that the 'savages' cannot give an adequate account of their own ideas, and that he, as an enlightened man of science, understands their beliefs better than they do. He accounts for the fetishism of taboo objects in the same way that, according to Adorno and Horkheimer, enlightened reason always exposes superstition: by unmasking it as 'anthropomorphism, the projection onto nature of the subjective'.[22] Freud announces that what the 'savages' fear is fear itself – 'objectified fear' (33) – which they have projected into an alien object. The savages provide another example of the superstitious tendency to make idols out of human ideas. In Freud, this fetishistic displacement of subjective processes into the objective world is called 'projection', and it is the defining characteristic of both the 'savage' and the civilized 'neurotic':

> The projection outwards of internal perceptions is a primitive mechanism, to which, for instance, our sense perceptions are subject, and which therefore normally plays a very large part in determining the form taken by our external world . . . internal perceptions of emotional and intellective processes can be projected outwards in the same way as sense perceptions; they are thus employed in building up the external world, though they should by rights remain part of the internal world.
>
> (81)

As usual in ideology, this fetishism misconstrues the relation of subject and object. The 'savage' and 'neurotic' minds are characterized by an extreme idealism; by the irrational belief that ideas alone can determine material events. The 'primitive' man mistreats an effigy of his enemy in the opinion that this will harm the real man; the 'neurotic' European feels compelled to perform a certain mechanical ritual to ward off misfortune. Each of them, according to Freud, mistakes 'an ideal connection for a real one' (104):

> Things become less important than ideas of things: whatever is done to the latter will inevitably also occur to the former. Relations which hold between the ideas of things are assumed to hold equally between the things themselves.
>
> (106)

The belief that ideas are present in the material world is characteristic of the primitive 'animism' which conceives of spirits inhabiting things. Freud provocatively adds that 'primitive peoples believe that human individuals are inhabited by similar spirits' (95), a notion which he scorns. As he was well aware, many people in Freud's own society still believed in such 'spirits' or 'souls'. But Freud puts his faith in the progress of human societies, from 'animism' through 'religion' to 'science' (110). This involves the progressive disengagement of ideas from the material world, until the scientific consciousness is able to analyse itself as just another object:

> primitive man transposed the structural conditions of his own mind into the external world; and we may attempt to reverse the process and put back into the human mind what animism teaches as to the nature of things.
>
> (114)

As Horkheimer and Adorno comment apropos of Freud's book, 'Animism spiritualized the object, whereas industrialism objectified the spirits of men'.[23] We can thus see that, although they move in opposite directions, 'savage' superstition and Freud's scientific method both insist on an illegitimate collapse of the subject/object dichotomy. The savages believe that their ideas can influence the material world, while Freud assumes that material experience creates our ideas. Freud's science is thus just as undialectical and metaphysical as the beliefs of the 'savages' to whom he condescends. Both these discourses are reductive; they both give priority to one side of the ideal/material binary, and they can therefore both be described as ideological modes of thought.

A CRISIS OF FAITH: STRUCTURALISM AND AFTER

In *Devil on the Cross* (1982), the Kenyan novelist Ngugi Wa Thiong'O offers a hilarious parody of capitalist ideology, as it is perceived by the bemused inhabitants of the neo-colonial world. This book combines a 'rational' critique of economic imperialism with a 'superstitious' subtext which associates it with the metaphysical forces of Evil. Ngugi's blend of realism and fantasy also allows him to retain the form and tone of conventional rationalizations of imperialism, while altering their content so as to reveal their real significance. Thus, at a 'Devil's Feast' held by 'Satan, the King of Hell' on behalf of the 'Organization for Modern Theft and Robbery', the Master of Ceremonies rises to announce:

> We who come from the developed world have had many years' experience of modern theft and robbery. I might also remind you that we are the owners of the houses and stores and granaries that contain all the money that has ever been snatched from the peoples of the world. You can see for yourselves that even our suits are made of bank notes. Today money is the ruler of all industry and commerce. Money is the *field marshal* of all the forces of theft and robbery on earth. *Money is supreme. Money rules the world.* . . . We believe in freedom, the freedom that allows one to rob and steal according to one's abilities.

> That's what we call *personal initiative* and *individual enterprise*.
> And that's why we have always stated that we belong to the
> *Free World*, a world where there are absolutely no barriers to
> stealing from others.[24]

This assumption that the wealth of Western civilization made it
intrinsically more advanced than the rest of the world grew to
seem increasingly dubious and self-interested over the course
of the twentieth century, and this was reflected in a series of
attempts to re-evaluate the relation of reason to irrational modes
of thought. The notions (which had been axiomatic since the
eighteenth century), that human history was characterized by
progress from a 'primitive' to a 'civilized' condition, and that
Europe was farther along that route than other parts of the world,
began to be challenged. One convincing theoretical rebuke to
Western pretensions was provided by the method of analysis known
as 'structuralism'. This discipline was inaugurated by the Swiss
linguist, Ferdinand de Saussure, whose lecture notes were collected
after his death as the *Course in General Linguistics* (1916). In out-
lining his definition of linguistics, Saussure pointedly refuses to
make any qualitative distinction between human languages:

> Linguistics takes for its data in the first instance all mani-
> festations of human language. Primitive peoples and civilized
> nations, early periods, classical periods, and periods of
> decadence, are all to be included.[25]

Saussure's method does not presuppose that 'civilized' languages
are the most sophisticated, or the best suited to the expression of
complicated ideas. He insists that synchronic and diachronic
linguistics must be kept separate, claiming that the study of a language's 'diachronic' development through time is a quite different
area from the analysis of its 'synchronic' structure at any particular
time. However, these two methods 'are not of equal importance.
It is clear that the synchronic point of view takes precedence over

the diachronic, since for the community of language users that is the one and only reality' (89).

What the synchronic approach reveals is the fact that words acquire meaning, not through any intrinsic correspondence with the objects they represent, but through their place within the linguistic structure. Saussure thus suggests that representation is autonomous and that, in fact, signs produce the objects they designate. He finds that this 'arbitrary nature of the sign' (68) pertains in every society:

> any means of expression accepted in a society rests in principle upon a collective habit, or on convention, which comes to the same thing. Signs of politeness, for instance, although often endowed with a certain natural expressiveness (prostrating oneself nine times on the ground is the way to greet an emperor in China) are none the less fixed by rule. It is this rule which renders them obligatory, not their intrinsic value.
>
> (ibid.)

Saussure's linguistics, then, indicates that meaning is arbitrarily produced out of a structured system of signs. This is an idea with extremely radical implications. If the significance which any given society attaches to certain signs is indeed a matter of arbitrary convention, then it becomes difficult for any particular society to claim that its ideas are inherently truer than those of any other, no matter how ostensibly primitive they may seem. What is more, Saussure presents his linguistics as a model for a much wider field of study:

> A language is a system of signs expressing ideas, and hence comparable to writing, the deaf-and-dumb alphabet, symbolic rites, forms of politeness, military signals, and so on. It is simply the most important of such systems. It is therefore possible to conceive of a science which studies the role of signs as part of social life. It would form part of social psychology, and hence

of general psychology. We shall call it semiology. . . . It would investigate the nature of signs and the laws governing them.

(15)

Saussure thus claims that all aspects of social life, to the degree that they are significant, are structured like a language. Since he believes that linguistic meaning is arbitrary, it therefore follows that all social behaviour is merely conventional. The inescapable conclusion is that, in the words of the structural anthropologist Claude Lévi-Strauss, 'man has always thought equally well', and that there can be no grounds for dismissing the thought systems of other societies as more 'primitive' than our own. In *The Savage Mind* (1962), Lévi-Strauss applies Saussure's method of analysis to the kinds of 'magical' systems which Freud studied in *Totem and Taboo*. As we might expect, he is led to very different conclusions. He refuses to call magic a more 'primitive' mode of thought than reason:

These are certainly not a function of different stages of the development of the human mind but rather of two strategic levels at which nature is accessible to scientific enquiry: one roughly adapted to that of perception and the imagination: the other at a remove from it.[26]

The characteristic of rational science is that it separates itself from the object studied, giving rise to the splits between subject and object, and between matter and spirit. Like Freud, Lévi-Strauss noted that 'primitive' societies do not operate through these dichotomies, but conceive of ideas as inherent in their objects. Unlike Freud, however, Lévi-Strauss does not regard this as a superstitious error; rather, he perceives in it an insight which the Enlightenment does not achieve until Hegel:

it is in this intransigent refusal on the part of the savage mind to allow anything human (or even living) to remain alien to it, that the real principle of dialectical reason is to be found.

(245)

'Primitive' societies, in other words, have not succumbed to the fatal divorce of subject and object which constitutes the central problem for Western philosophy. Of course, for Marx this split is itself illusory, and testifies to a mode of fetishism which is no less superstitious than the animistic world view. We might say that where capitalism objectifies the subject, animism subjectifies the object. The result is a strange convergence between ostensibly distinct modes of thought, so that animistic beliefs can be used to make sense of the ideological effects produced by market capitalism. In *The Devil and Commodity Fetishism* (1980), Michael Taussig examines the response of South American peasants to encroaching capitalism, and finds that they can easily interpret the changes in their lives within their pre-existent systems of thought. The places where the newly proletarianized peasants work, and the products of their labour, are invested with the properties which were associated with the evil spirits, or 'devils', of their 'superstitious' religions. As Taussig demonstrates, this is a perfectly comprehensible transposition:

> If we 'thingify' parts of a living system, ignore the context of which they are part, and then observe that the things move . . . as though they were alive . . . reification leads to fetishization. . . . The devil in the Bolivian tin mines offers spellbinding testimony to the fidelity with which people can capture the transformation of fetishization while subjecting it to a paganism that will capture it.[27]

Structuralist linguistics and anthropology, then, opened up the possibility of studying the constitutive role of ideology. All societies represent and give meaning to the lives of their inhabitants by constructing systems of ideas about them. These systems are not optional extras, but constitute the lived reality of the people. Thus, the ideological representations by which we, in advanced capitalist countries, bestow significance on our surroundings, are by no means 'natural' but are instances of the Aristotelian, man-made 'second nature'. It is characteristic of ideology, however, for this second nature to pass itself off as the 'first' nature, so that what has been constructed by human beings is fetishistically regarded as eternal and unchangeable.

The danger for structural analyses of signs is that, by focusing on the formal relations between the various elements of linguistic or semiotic codes, they will exclude or render nugatory the influence exercised on these signifying systems by external reality. Post-structuralist theory often takes the autonomous, constitutive role of representation for granted, or even celebrates it as a ludic liberation from dour referentiality. A salutary warning against this tendency was sounded in one of the earliest responses to Saussure, V.N. Volosinov's *Marxism and the Philosophy of Language* (1929). Volosinov attacks Saussure's assumption that the structure of language is inherently imprinted on the human mind, and he points out the heritage of this idea in Cartesian rationalism:

> The idea of the conventionality, the arbitrariness, of language is a typical one for rationalism as a whole. . . . What interests the mathematically minded rationalists is not the relationship of the sign to the actual reality it reflects or to the individual who is its originator, but the relationship of sign to sign within a closed system already accepted and authorized. In other words, they are interested only in the inner logic of the system of signs itself, taken, as in algebra, completely independently of the meanings that give signs their content.[28]

Saussure and his followers, that is to say, cannot account for either the individual subjective origin or the objective referent of signs. Like Descartes, Saussure suggests that the material world is constructed by certain universal properties of the human mind. In Volosinov's view, this ignores the interdependence of ideas, signs and things. His own description of signification locates it at the intersection of subject and object; it consists in a subjective significance being read into a material thing:

> any physical body may be perceived as an image.... Any
> such artistic-symbolic image to which a particular physical
> object gives rise is already an ideological product. The physical
> object is converted into a sign. Without ceasing to be a part of
> material reality, such an object, to some degree, reflects and
> refracts another reality.
>
> (9)

This 'other reality' Volosinov calls 'the domain of signs', which is 'the ideological sphere' (10). 'Ideology' inhabits the realm of representation; it is an extra, subjective significance, which is added on to the material world by the observer. This act of giving symbolic significance to a material object is analogous to Simmel's description of the formation of value: it involves the manifestation of subjective processes in the objective world. Representation is thus neither objective nor subjective; it is the third term in which the two poles of the dichotomy meet. This is what allows Volosinov to equate representation with ideology, which must be embodied in material practices, but which, *contra* Althusser, nevertheless retains a subjective dimension. Thus Volosinov criticizes the polarizing, essentialist tendencies of idealism and materialism alike. In these approaches, he says, 'The individual consciousness . . . becomes either all or nothing':

> For idealism it has become all: its locus is somewhere above
> existence and it determines the latter.... For psychological
> positivism, on the contrary, consciousness amounts to nothing:
> it is just a conglomeration of fortuitous, psychophysiological
> reactions which, by some miracle, results in meaningful and
> unified ideological creativity.... However, the ideological, as
> such, cannot possibly be explained in terms of either of these
> superhuman or subhuman, animalian, roots. Its real place in
> existence is in the special, social material of signs created by
> man.
>
> (12)

The analysis of this process of constructing ideological meaning, as was foretold by Saussure, has come to be known as semiology.

One of the earliest and most successful attempts to apply this rigorous 'science of signs' was undertaken by Roland Barthes, in *Mythologies* (1957). As the title implies, this book is an anthropology of contemporary French society, which Barthes believes contains a system of modern 'myths' no less extensive, constitutive or superstitious than those held by ancient or 'primitive' peoples. He is interested in the ways in which certain social phenomena are invested with a significance which is at once arbitrary and universally understood, and which, as he says, serves the interests of the 'bourgeois' class. For example:

> I am at the barber's, and a copy of *Paris-Match* is offered to me. On the cover, a young Negro in a French uniform is saluting, with his eyes uplifted, probably fixed on a fold of the tricolor. All this is the meaning of the picture. But, whether naively or not, I see very well what it signifies to me: that France is a great Empire, that all her sons, without any color discrimination, faithfully serve under her flag, and that there is no better answer to the detractors of an alleged colonialism than the zeal shown by this Negro in serving his so-called oppressors.[29]

A fairly complex political and historical point is thus established by the judicious use of bare images. It is the function of such 'mythology', according to Barthes, to make contingent, historical phenomena appear as though they were natural, and thus inevitable. Of course, it would be very difficult to win an argument about the virtues of colonialism by simply pointing to this picture. That is not the point. Such representations are not supposed to be amenable to reasoned proof or rebuttal: this is why Barthes says that they work on the level of myth. In our society, representations of this kind have nevertheless become more effective in moulding people's opinions than rational persuasion: think, for example, of today's methods of political campaigning. The mythological elements of Enlightenment have finally cast aside the mask of reason, and step proudly into the spotlight.

There is really nothing new in this mode of ideological indoctrination: Marx discusses a similar use of representation in *The Eighteenth Brumaire*. However, it may well be that the development of technological apparatuses, the extent of mass communications, and the increased research into marketing and advertising techniques, have established this mythical use of representation on a firmer basis today than ever before. Representation becomes indistinguishable from reality to the degree that the commodity form obscures the true nature of things. One way of defining 'the postmodern condition' is as the state of mind which results from the final triumph of the commodity, the ultimate victory of exchange-value, and thus the elevation of representation over reality. In the final chapter, we will need to consider whether it makes any kind of sense to describe such a universal consciousness as 'false'. Or, to put the question another way: have we reached the 'end of ideology'?

6

POSTMODERNISM

living people have become bits of ideology.
                                    Theodor Adorno[1]

No more ideology, only simulacra.
                                    Jean Baudrillard[2]

NIETZSCHE: THE PRECURSOR

Friedrich Nietzsche is the major nineteenth-century source for the ideas which characterize today's postmodern condition. In particular, the ethical and epistemological relativism of the postmodern world, its scepticism about the possibility of distinguishing truth from falsehood, finds its prototype in Nietzsche's radically nihilistic thought. In *On the Genealogy of Morals* (1887), Nietzsche sets out to subvert the most deeply held pieties of the 'enlightened' Western world, by speculating about the origins of Judaeo-Christian morality and of rational Greek philosophy. Both these pillars of civilization ultimately rest, according to Nietzsche, on a single foundation:

> Greek thinking begins with and for a long time holds to the proposition that mankind is divided into 'good' and 'bad', and these terms are quite as much social, political, and economic as they are moral. . . . The dichotomy is absolute and exclusive for a simple reason: it began as the aristocrats' view of society and reflects their idea of the gulf between them-selves and the 'others'.[3]

With arresting cynicism, Nietzsche declares that the entire tradition of Western philosophy can be traced to a self-interested legitimation of hierarchical power-structures. In Chapter 1 we saw how Aristotle deduces the need for the domination of certain people by others from the hierarchy between ideas and matter. Here, Nietzsche contends that the original purpose of the binary opposition between good and bad is to justify and perpetuate the division of society into a privileged group of Greek, aristocratic men, and the excluded 'others': women, slaves and barbarians. The dichotomy rationalizes this situation, making it appear natural and reasonable. And yet it also forms the very basis of rational thought, which proceeds by positing such binary opposites and resolving them in syntheses. The whole of Western philosophy is thus originally an ideology, in so far as it is a ruse designed to serve the interests of a particular group of people.

As one might expect, those excluded from the exalted circle of rulers frequently felt aggrieved at their position. As Nietzsche puts it, the oppressed experienced a sense of '*ressentiment*'. This French word translates into English as 'resentment', but it also carries stronger connotations of hatred and desire for revenge. This desire was expressed, according to Nietzsche, in theological Judaism:

> It was the Jews who, with awe-inspiring consistency, dared to invert the aristocratic value-equation (good=noble=powerful= beautiful=happy=beloved of God) and to hang on to this inver-sion with their teeth, the teeth of the most abysmal hatred (the

hatred of impotence), saying 'the wretched alone are the good; the poor, impotent, lowly alone are the good; the suffering, deprived, sick, ugly alone are pious, alone are blessed by God, blessedness is for them alone – and you, the powerful and noble, are on the contrary the evil, the cruel, the lustful, the insatiable, the godless to all eternity; and you shall be in all eternity the unblessed, accursed, and damned!'

(34)

Of course, the message which Nietzsche attributes to 'the Jews' is also delivered by Christ in the Sermon on the Mount, and Christianity is the real target of Nietzsche's wrath. The greatest confidence-trick in history, he claims, took place when the wretched of the earth were able to turn the tables, and pass off their own empirical qualities – humility, poverty, meekness, suffering – as universally positive values. With the rise to prevalence of this Judaeo-Christian morality, the dichotomy good/bad is transmuted into an opposition between good and evil, with the latter denoting the characteristics of the oppressors: pride, power, aggression and luxury.

Many people would argue that this 'transvaluation of values' constitutes the greatest achievement of human history. But Nietzsche is infuriated by his discovery that Western morality has its origins in primitive impulses to revenge and destruction, and he takes this as evidence of his civilization's unmitigated hypocrisy. Having kicked away the foundation, he glories in the total collapse of the edifice. Among the wreckage are such chimeras as the individual self, or 'subject', which Nietzsche holds to be merely an effect of the grammatical first person singular combined with the hierarchical, binary structure of reason, which presupposes that there must be a subject where there is an object:

A quantum of force is equal to a quantum of drive, will, effect – more, it is nothing other than precisely this very driving, willing, effecting, and only owing to the seduction of language (and of the fundamental errors of reason that are petrified in it) which conceives and misconceives all effects as conditioned by something that causes effects, by a 'subject,' can it appear otherwise ... there is no 'being' behind doing, effecting, becoming; 'the doer' is merely a fiction added to the deed – the deed is everything.

(45)

The belief in an autonomous self is one of the fundamental characteristics of the Western 'metaphysics' which Nietzsche despises. His extreme scepticism drives him to debunk all such metaphors of depth, which assume that human history and human life have some deep, underlying significance or final meaning – the suggestion that ideology is the reflection of a material base, for example, or the notion that the material world is a manifestation of ideal forms, would be anathema to Nietzsche. He envisages the imposition of such hierarchies on the world as an act of aggression, the manifestation of the will to power.

For instance, Nietzsche traces the origin of such subjective qualities as memory and guilt to the demand of creditors that debtors should be accountable for their debts. With a character-istic appeal to German etymology, he claims that 'the major moral concept *Schuld* [guilt] has its origin in the very material concept *Schulden* [debts]' (62–3). All legal theories of guilt and punish-ment, 'the idea that every injury has its *equivalent* and can actually be paid back, even if only through the *pain* of the culprit' (63), rest upon 'the contractual relationship between *creditor* and *debtor*, which is as old as the idea of "legal subjects" and in turn points back to the fundamental forms of buying, selling, barter, trade, and traffic' (ibid.). Nietzsche differs from Marx in many respects, but they share the belief that an exchange-based economy constructs a false kind of subject, by imposing on it an illusory equivalence with the objective sphere. Nietzsche recalls how, in the ancient world, the creditor could inflict every kind of indignity and torture upon the body of the debtor; for example, cut from it as much as seemed commensurate with the size of the debt – and everywhere and from early times one had exact evaluations, *legal* evaluations, of the individual limbs and parts of the body from this point of view, some of them going into horrible and minute detail.

(64)

In Shakespeare's *The Merchant of Venice*, Shylock assumes just such an equivalence between the pound of Antonio's flesh to which he is legally entitled and the debt he is owed. It is notable that Shakespeare associates Shylock with every kind of objectification. As a Jew, he is linked to the 'fleshly' dispensation of the Old Testament; he puts his faith in justice and the human law rather than in divine redemption; his avarice ties him to the material things of this world; and he is constantly figured in terms of death and the flesh, as when the play's Christians refer to him as 'old carrion'. However, Nietzsche might point out that Shylock is at least honest about the objectifying effects of finance: he does not bother to conceal his reified assumptions behind the hypocritical platitudes of Christianity.

Like Althusser, Nietzsche contends that the individual subject can only maintain its integrity through its faith in an absolute subject. This originary, seminal entity is the *logos*, the ultimate source of all meaning and truth. Thus Nietzsche remarks that we are still deluded by 'the Christian faith, which was also Plato's, that God is truth, that truth is *divine*' (152). This faith, in his view, will not trouble us much longer. What, he eagerly speculates, would happen 'if God himself turns out to be our *longest lie*?' (ibid.). It is the task of Nietzsche's philosophy to answer this question, to criticize the 'will to truth' which he sees as the cause of hierarchy and oppression, and to raise the revolutionary possibility that truth may not, finally, even be a good thing.

Depending on which way you look at it, Nietzsche can be seen either as abolishing the concept of ideology, or as expanding it to include all Western thought. False consciousness can only be identified by comparison with some standard of truth. But according to Nietzsche, the belief in an ultimate truth is in fact the 'longest lie'. All philosophy since Plato has been logocentric; centred on the illusion of an absolute source and guarantor of meaning. Since Nietzsche believes that he has unmasked this illusion as a disguise for base and selfish interests, and thus as facilitating domination and oppression, it would seem that there is no consciousness which is not false, and that the notion of 'ideology' has thus become meaningless and obsolete.

MICHEL FOUCAULT: *DEUS ABSCONDITUS*

The work of Michel Foucault blends Nietzschean history with poststructuralist linguistics; a combination which has come to define philosophical 'postmodernism'. In *The Order of Things* (1966), Foucault identifies two major eras in the history of the human sciences: the 'classical' phase, running from 1660 to 1800; and the 'modern' epoch, which begins with the nineteenth century and which, according to Foucault's apocalyptic pronouncement, is drawing to a close even as he writes. His contention is that, during each of these periods, such disciplines as biology, linguistics and economics shared a common 'well-defined regularity', and obeyed 'the laws of a certain code of knowledge'.[4] It is with this 'code' that Foucault is concerned, and this fact may lead an innocent reader to assume that he is engaged in an essentially structuralist project. Foucault's neurotically vehement denial of this characterization (xiv) indicates that it contains some truth. But, whereas the first generation of structuralists such as Saussure and Lévi-Strauss conceived of 'deep' structures underlying their material manifestations in a metaphysical fashion, Foucault is interested in the specific, concrete results of these abstract 'rules of formation'. He takes Nietzsche's aphorism that there is no subject, no 'doer', that 'the deed is everything', as his methodological basis.

It is immediately clear that there is no room in such an approach for the concept of 'ideology'. Foucault is an ultra-materialist: he refuses to admit the existence of any 'ideal' sphere. It is significant in this regard that Foucault was a pupil of Althusser, whose reductive materialism was discussed earlier. However, Althusser retained the notion of ideology as false consciousness, essentially equating it with idealism. For Foucault, it is no longer possible to use terms such as 'true', 'false', or even 'consciousness' in any absolute sense. There have been 'discourses' which have given rise to 'truth-effects', but the very fact that they have been produced by human beings is enough, for Foucault as for Nietzsche, to deprive them of any objectively veridical character. Similarly, there are institutions and practices – the family, the school, the church – which function so as to produce the sense that we are individual subjects with independent consciousnesses, but this effect is neither eternal nor inevitable.

What are real are the sets of rules, the patterns of classification, which allow us to make sense of the chaotic wealth of empirical data which daily rushes in on us from all sides. It is Foucault's desire to confront his culture with

> the stark fact that there exists, below the level of its spontaneous orders, things that are themselves capable of being ordered, that belong to a certain unspoken order; the fact, in short, that order exists.
>
> (xx)

It is this ultimate 'order', the 'conditions of possibility' (xxii) for knowledge at any given historical moment, which allows us to make sense of the world. This is clearly a Kantian position, and Foucault acknowledges this when he says that he is concerned to discover the 'historical a priori' of the classical and modern human sciences. Unlike Kant, however, Foucault emphasizes the historical aspect – where Kant wanted to identify the conditions which make possible experience in general, Foucault is interested in what allows the formation of particular, historically specific types of knowledge. He wants, as he puts it, to study the process which 'makes manifest the modes of being of order'. But it is difficult to escape the conclusion that Foucault's 'order' is a transcendent, determining entity, albeit one which is never fully present in the world. It is, in fact, a twentieth-century version of *deus absconditus*, the departed god who governs our actions without being fully manifest to us.

The philosophical implications of Foucault's method in *The Order of Things* are so intriguing that they rather overshadow his contentious readings of actual historical discourses. Foucault seems to acknowledge this by dedicating his next important work, *The Archaeology of Knowledge* (1969), to an exposition of methodological problems. His declared aim is to escape from the teleological, totalizing, subject-centred approach, which has dominated Western philosophy since Plato; he rebels against the notion that history is a narrative acted out by a coherent subject:

> Making historical analysis the discourse of the continuous and making human consciousness the original subject of all historical development and all action are the two sides of the same system of thought.[5]

When we try to shape the flux of events into a coherent narrative, according to Foucault, we impose upon it the ostensibly unified, apparently conscious form of our own subjectivity. In fact, however, the subject is neither unified nor fully conscious: it can only come to appear so when it is artificially removed from the objective context which generates it. This is the source of idealism, the philosophy which illegitimately imposes an ideal order on material reality. Foucault is opposed, above all, to the notion of 'spirit', which enables us to establish between the simultaneous or successive phenomena of a given period a community of meanings, symbolic links, an interplay of resemblance and reflexion, or which allows the sovereignty of collective consciousness to emerge as the principle of unity and explanation.

(22)

What is being attacked here is the Hegelian concept of an ideal sphere whose developing relationship with the material dimension guides and moulds the course of history. However, Foucault does not suggest that, in the absence of a coherent narrative of history, events are purely random and indeterminate. On the contrary, his notion of 'discourse' is rigidly determinist. In identifying a discourse, he writes, 'we must show why it could not be other than it was, in what respect it is exclusive of any other, how it assumes . . . a place that no other could occupy' (28). His objection is to the notion that a discourse is formed by any 'spiritual' or 'ideal' influences. On the other hand, Foucault is also concerned to distance his work from the naive empiricism which assumes that we can have unmediated access to the material world. As he puts it, he aims 'To substitute for the enigmatic treasure of "things" anterior to discourse, the regular formation of objects that emerge only in discourse' (47).

It thus seems that, like such dialectical thinkers as Hegel and Marx, Foucault is attempting to transcend the polarity between idealism and materialism. But Foucault rejects the dialectic, portraying it in Nietzschean terms as a tyrannical imposition of human logic on the recalcitrant blur of reality. As we saw in the case of Althusser, any non-dialectical attempt to abolish the idea/matter opposition risks reducing one pole of the dichotomy to the other – declaring either that matter is, in reality, an idea (as with Berkeley); or that ideas are, in fact, material (as with Hume). Foucault sometimes suggests that his realm of 'discourse' occupies a middle ground between these binary alternatives:

> We shall not return to the state anterior to discourse – in which
> nothing has yet been said, and in which things are only just
> beginning to emerge out of the grey light; and we shall not pass
> beyond discourse in order to discover the forms that it has
> created and left behind it; we shall remain, or try to remain, at
> the level of discourse itself.

(48)

As soon as Foucault offers a precise definition of the term
'discourse', however, this balance begins to collapse. Thus, he
announces that 'We shall call discourse a group of statements in so
far as they belong to the same discursive formation' (117). But
when we ask what a 'statement' is, we are told that

> it must have a material existence. Could one speak of a state-
> ment if a voice had not articulated it, if a surface did not bear
> its signs, if it had not become embodied in a sense-perceptible
> element. . . . Could one speak of a statement as an ideal, silent
> figure? The statement is always given through some material
> medium.

(100)

In order to exist 'for us', the 'statement' must take on a material
form. A 'discourse' is a regular pattern, or 'formation', of such
'statements'. To all intents and purposes, then, 'discourse' is itself
material. And yet Foucault has already positioned discourse as the
factor which mediates between the ideal and the material. We can
thus see that the attempt to find a third term has failed. Like
Althusser, like Freud and, beyond them, like the *philosophes* of
the French Enlightenment, Foucault can only move beyond the
ideal/material dichotomy by collapsing one of its terms into
the other, and he too arrives at the familiar position of materialist
determinism.

In his later work, Foucault concerns himself less with 'discourse',
and more with 'power'. Like discourse, power is always already
material, and in texts such as *Discipline and Punish* (1975), power

is ascribed the role of moulding the subject itself. Not only is the subject ultimately material (and thus, in effect, an object), but it is formed out of a process of subjection to a dominating power. The notion of 'ideology' as false consciousness is therefore necessarily redundant, for two reasons. First, it refers to 'consciousness', which is not material and therefore not real; and second, it assumes the possibility of falsehood, a concept which can have no meaning if the thinking subject is itself merely the objective product of power. There is nothing to be regretted in the dominance of power (it could not be shown to rest on false assumptions), since it is that power which creates the very individuals who recognize it as power.

It would thus seem that 'power' is a quasi-divine force for Foucault. However, he is careful to avoid a 'logocentric' description of power, which would discover a single, central source from which it flows – God, the King, or the bourgeoisie, for example. In the first volume of *The History of Sexuality*, Foucault gives the following account of power:

> Power's condition of possibility . . . must not be sought in the primary existence of a central point, in a unique source of sovereignty from which secondary and descendent forms would emanate; it is the moving substrate of force relations which, by virtue of their inequality, constantly engender states of power, but the latter are always local and unstable. The omnipresence of power: not because it has the privilege of consolidating everything under its invincible unity, but because it is produced from one moment to the next, at every point, or rather in every relation from one point to another. Power is everywhere; not because it embraces everything, but because it comes from everywhere.[6]

What, then, is this ubiquitous 'power' which creates all human subjects? The facile answer would be that it is simply another surrogate for the religious Creator; a *deus absconditus* who has deserted Heaven the better to incarnate himself throughout his creation. Some evidence for this is provided in *Discipline and Punish*, where Foucault suggests that the paradigmatic institution of the modern world is the prison. He refers in particular to Jeremy Bentham's design for a 'panopticon': a central control tower, from which the guards would be able to look into every cell at once. The implication is that today's individuals have internalized this system of surveillance, so that instead of submitting to the external strictures of a judging God, we now practice a self-discipline which is the residue of the dead religious morality. F. Scott Fitzgerald makes a similar point in *The Great Gatsby*, when he employs the gaze emanating from an advertising billboard as a symbol for the departed God, whose silent condemnation of the amoral lives of the protagonists persists even after His disappearance. But if it is true that Foucault's 'power' is an internalized God we are in deep trouble, for it is a notably cruel and malign force.[7] This must be so because he insists on limiting its scope to the material world; refusing the possibility of an ideal dimension in which the material world's manifest injustices might be explained or comprehended. In *Power/Knowledge* (1980), he declares

> I'm not one of those who try to elicit the effects of power at the level of ideology. Indeed I wonder whether, before one poses the question of ideology, it wouldn't be more materialist to study first the question of the body and the effects of power on it.[8]

Undoubtedly it would be more materialist, though the fact that Foucault takes this as in itself sufficient reason for following this course indicates that his materialism is ultimately dogmatic and metaphysical. As a result, the conflicts and issues which earlier philosophy discussed under the rubric of 'ideology' are simply internalized. The claim that 'The individual is an effect of power' (98) implies that power should be analysed within the individual. Thus Foucault is led into such ostensibly 'idealist' declarations as 'we all have a fascism in our heads' (99). When an interviewer asks

Foucault about wider social conflicts – 'who ultimately, in your view, are the subjects who oppose each other?' (208) – his reply is startling:

> This is just a hypothesis, but I would say it's all against all. There aren't immediately given subjects of the struggle, one the proletariat, the other the bourgeoisie. Who fights against whom? We all fight each other. *And there is always within each of us something that fights something else.*
>
> (ibid., emphasis added)

Are we so far away, here, from the traditional religious conception of the subject as the site of a battle between the cosmic powers of sin and righteousness? We saw earlier how the Frankfurt School applied Lukács's analysis of commodity fetishism so as to understand the 'class struggle' as a fight enacted within each individual consciousness. As Foucault admits, he only became aware of the work of Adorno, Horkheimer and Marcuse 'when I was no longer at the age of making intellectual "discoveries"'.[9] With disarming modesty, Foucault defers to the Frankfurt School, while maintaining that his own work is very similar to theirs:

> Now, obviously, if I had been familiar with the Frankfurt School, if I had been aware of it at the time, I would not have said a number of stupid things that I did say and I would have avoided many of the detours which I made while trying to pursue my own humble path – when, meanwhile, avenues had been opened up by the Frankfurt School. It is a strange case of non-penetration between two very similar types of thinking which is explained, perhaps, by that very similarity.[10]

Certainly there are some similarities between the Frankfurt and the Foucauldian traditions – the critique of reason as an instrument of oppression and the consequent sense of 'a fascism in our heads' is the most obvious one. But there are also important differences. First, the Frankfurt School remain aggressively dialectical thinkers:

it is hard to imagine Adorno reducing the ideal to the material as does Foucault. Second, their thought is based upon Lukács's concept of reification, which in turn is founded upon Marx's anatomy of the commodity in the opening chapter of *Capital*. In contrast, Foucault's work lacks any analysis of commodity fetishism, and he is therefore ultimately driven into a species of the quasi-religious metaphysics which he purports to deplore.

DEBORD AND BAUDRILLARD

Foucault's protestations to the contrary notwithstanding,[11] the Lukácsian analysis of the commodity was current in some French intellectual circles during the 1960s. It offered a way of understanding what Foucault merely records: the fact that the traditional division between the ideal and the material realms is becoming confused and displaced. In *Society of the Spectacle* (1967), Guy Debord announces the 'materialization of ideology',[12] in the form of the 'spectacle', which 'is ideology *par excellence*' (215). We have seen how, in *Capital*, Marx claims that commodity exchange involves the recognition in one object of the image, the representation, of another object, with which it is to be exchanged. When this image is believed to be objectively present within the body of the first object, we have reached the stage of commodity fetishism. This objectified representation is then generalized in the form of money, the universal commodity which secretly represents alienated human activity. In Lukács, this commodity fetishism gives rise to the ideological phenomenon of 'reification', which consists in seeing people as if they were things, while simultaneously attributing a spectral life and ghostly agency to objects. The relationship between the ideal and the material is distorted, and this distortion can be traced to a fundamental belief in the illusory autonomy of representation.

Debord's argument is that, fifty years after Lukács's *History and Class-consciousness*, representation has become autonomous *in fact*.

Such is the extent and power of commodity fetishism by 1967 that
it no longer makes sense to refer to it as an illusion. The result,
according to Debord, is the complete dominance of representation
– the 'spectacle' – over what had been thought of as 'reality':

> This is the principle of *commodity fetishism*, the domination of
> society by 'intangible as well as tangible things', which reaches
> its absolute fulfillment in the spectacle, where the tangible
> world is replaced by a selection of images which exist above it,
> and which at the same time are recognized as the tangible *par
> excellence*.
>
> (36)

In the consumer societies of the late twentieth century, exchange-
value (a purely symbolic form) has become more real, more
objective, than use-value (a material phenomenon). Objects are
conceived, designed and produced for the purpose of making
money by selling them, rather than for reasons of practical utility.
Vast resources are devoted to manipulating the consciousnesses of
consumers, and stimulating in them desires which can be met by
the acquisition of commodities. As we have seen, to view an object
as a commodity is to perceive it very differently from when we see
it merely as something to be used. In our society consumers do not
buy their clothes, cars, or even their food, for their use-values
alone. Rather, they see in these objects symbolic significances,
which determine their patterns of consumption. These patterns in
turn dictate the movements of the stock, bond and currency
exchanges, and these movements exert a profound influence on the
material lives of people all over the world. So the symbolic realm,
the realm of representation, literally does determine what goes on
in the material world.

Of course, human beings have always attached 'extra', symbolic
significance to the objects around them. But the complete
dominance of the market, of the exchange of commodities, in
today's world economy is unprecedented. Given the Marxian

and Lukácsian accounts of the effects of commodification on consciousness, this is a cause for serious concern. Debord notes that, to the degree that commodification becomes dominant in a society, an illusory significance, a false appearance, is imposed upon the real world, or the thing-in-itself. The result is a massive distortion of the relationships between ideas, matter and represen- tation. As a Marxist, Debord believes that capital represent objectified labour. Furthermore, 'The spectacle is *capital* to such a degree of accumulation that it becomes an image' (34). The thing-in-itself is obscured by its form of appearance. But the thing- in-itself in this case is *ourselves* – human labour, human activity and therefore human life itself, which is hidden and dominated by its simultaneously objectified and symbolic form of appearance: capital.

In a commodity culture, then, we can expect that the human subject will be objectified. What is more, 'When the real world changes into simple images, simple images become real beings and effective motivations of a hypnotic behavior' (18). The commodi- ties themselves, being fetishized, are ascribed an active power. So Debord's 'society of the spectacle' systematically objectifies the subject, and subjectifies the object. Clearly, this is about as false as consciousness can possibly get. But Debord's point is precisely that the triumph of commodification renders the notion of false consciousness obsolete. We are faced, as he says, with 'the materialization of ideology. Society has become what ideology already was' (217). The dreadful truth Debord wants his readers to confront is that a way of thinking which is demonstrably erroneous and harmful is nonetheless an objectively accurate account of a real, material situation.

Debord thus arrives at much the same conclusions as Nietzsche and Foucault. It no longer makes sense to talk of a human 'subject', representation has become autonomous, history has no ultimate end or meaning, there is no way of distinguishing truth from false- hood or appearance from reality, and so on. But Debord has reached this position by a different route. His Marxist assumption that the roots of historical change can be traced to the economy leads him to study the 'postmodern condition' in relation to the predominant form of economic activity in postmodern society – commodity exchange. Since he views such activity as based on systematic error and exploitation, he inevitably sees the consumer society as an infernal, fallen condition, in which human beings fetishize the products of their own activity and, in the form of the market, give them absolute power over their lives.

Against this characterization, one might argue that the postmodern world has merely freed us from the repressive effects of Enlightenment reason. Following Nietzsche, one might claim that binary logic, metaphors of depth, the absolute subject, and teleological history, are in fact instruments of hierarchy and tools of oppression. This, more or less, is the position espoused by Foucault, Derrida, Lyotard, and also currently by Jean Baudrillard. Baudrillard's career is especially interesting, for he began as an associate of Debord and the Situationist movement, lamenting the effects of commodification on consciousness. Since the mid-1970s, however, Baudrillard has shifted his attitude, so that he currently appears to take a more benign view of postmodern society.

In *For a Critique of the Political Economy of the Sign* (1972), Baudrillard elaborates on Debord's incisive but brusque analysis of the way commodification influences signification. To do so, he modifies the semiotic theory of Saussure, whom we discussed in the previous chapter. Saussure claimed that a linguistic sign was made up of two elements: the 'signifier', which was the sign's material form, and the 'signified', which was the concept evoked by the signifier. Baudrillard's argument is that '*the logic of the commodity and of political economy is at the very heart of the sign*, in the abstract equation of signifier and signified'.[13] Commodification and signification both depend on the recognition of an abstract equivalence, either between the objects to be exchanged, or between the internal elements of the sign. In consumer society, this abstract equivalence departs from its previous, humble, enabling role, and steps forth to claim its inheritance. The signified collapses into the signifier; the concept disappears beneath its representation. Following Debord, Baudrillard describes this process as the materialization, the incarnation, of false consciousness: 'Nor is ideology some Imaginary floating in the wake of exchange value: it is the very operation of exchange value itself' (169).

Baudrillard sees his own work as 'decoding the birth of the sign form in the same way that Marx was able to uncover the birth of the commodity form' (112). Marxists, he notes, have not taken account of the autonomy of representation:

> Marxist analysis today finds itself in the same position with respect to the field of ideology as the bourgeois economists before (and since) Marx vis a vis material production: the real source of value and the real process of production are skipped over. It is from neglect of this social labour of sign production that ideology derives its transcendence; signs and culture appear enveloped in a 'fetishism,' a mystery equivalent to, and contemporaneous with that of the commodity.
>
> (115)

At this stage, Baudrillard portrays the autonomy of representation as the result of false consciousness. Signs have become divorced from their referents because exchange-value has triumphed over use-value; this phenomenon is definitive of consumer society. Thus 'The definition of an object of consumption is entirely independent of the objects themselves and *exclusively a function of the logic of significations*' (67). If this is the case, then the opposition between ideas and matter no longer holds:

> Marx demonstrated that the objectivity of material production did not reside in its materiality, but in its form. . . . The same

analytical reduction must be applied to ideology: its objectivity does not reside in its 'ideality', that is, in a realist metaphysic of thought contents, but in its form.

(144)

'Ideology', for Baudrillard, transcends the artificial, essentialist dichotomy of material and ideal. There is a 'simultaneity of the ideological operation on the level of psychic structure and social structure' (100), and 'the operation amounts to defining the subject by means of the object and the object in terms of the subject' (71). Thus, 'just as concrete work is abstracted . . . into labour power' (83) in early forms of capitalist economies, so in consumer society, 'desire is abstracted and atomized into needs, in order to make it homogeneous with the means of satisfaction (products, images, sign-objects, etc.) and thus to multiply consummativity' (ibid.). This latter concept of 'consummativity' replaces 'productivity' as the organizing principle of consumer capitalism. Just as labour-power abstracts human activity, consummativity abstracts the human spirit. To make a person into a consumer, it is necessary to tamper with his personality, to create and implant new needs and desires within him. And this manipulation of the soul is just as necessary to the functioning of today's economy as the disciplining and regimentation of the body was to the capitalism of the industrial epoch.

To the extent that the needs and aspirations of the postmodern subject are artificially created to serve the interests of the market economy, one can say that the subject has ceased to have any meaningful independent existence. Baudrillard does not hesitate to declare that 'The individual is an ideological structure. . . . The individual is nothing but the subject thought in economic terms' (133). Today's chimerical individual is merely an alibi, necessary to the functioning of consummativity. Baudrillard is able to demonstrate that this is true of the subject in consumer society, but he extends the scope of his argument to suggest that there has never been an authentic human subject. In that case, the question arises of why there is anything actually wrong with the consumer society. If the individual has never existed, then nothing is lost when the subject is objectified. If objects have always genuinely lorded it over subjects, then it makes no sense to argue that commodification bestows upon them an illusory, fetishistic power. If the notion of 'consciousness' is false, how can there be such a thing as 'false consciousness'? Baudrillard's summary of the course of his own investigations is apt: 'we started by meddling with received ideas about fetishism, only to discover that the whole theory of ideology may be in doubt' (90).

In *The Mirror of Production* (1973), Baudrillard rereads Marx in the light of these postmodern circumstances. He finds that, in his 'critique of political economy', Marx retained many of the fundamental presuppositions of the capitalist system which he criticized. For example, Marx assumes a human essence which is alienated in the labour process, as well as a use-value inherent in the object, which is obscured in the process of exchange. While possibly valid for early capitalism, such essentialist concepts are not applicable to the consumer age, in which representation has become autonomous and non-referential:

> The super-ideology of the sign and the general operationaliz-
> ation of the signifier – everywhere sanctioned today by the new
> master disciplines of structural linguistics, semiology, inform-
> ation theory and cybernetics – has replaced good old political
> economy as the theoretical basis of the system. . . . Here there
> is a revolution of the capitalist system equal in importance to the
> industrial revolution.[14]

Baudrillard argues that Saussurian linguistics is ideological, because it retains a concrete referent, located outside the sign, just as Marx retains an essential use-value, distinct from exchange-value. 'In fact', he says, 'the use value of labor power does not exist any more than the use value of products or the autonomy of signified and referent' (30). Exchange-value produces the illusion of use-value to serve its own ends, as the signifier produces the illusion that it necessarily refers to a particular signified. These 'concrete' phenomena are merely the 'ideological ectoplasm' which ground the systems of exchange and signification in a hallucinatory 'reality'.

Baudrillard here defines 'ideology' as referentiality: the belief that signs point to something beyond themselves, that there is a depth beneath the surface. In a suggestive passage from *Simulations* (1983), he recalls the struggles over religious images, which were discussed in Chapter 1. Idolatry, as he notes, poses the question of the nature of signification in a particularly apposite form:

> what becomes of the divinity when it reveals itself in icons, when it is multiplied in simulacra? Does it remain the supreme authority, simply incarnated in images as a visible theology? Or is it volatilized into simulacra which alone deploy the pomp and power of fascination – the visible machinery of icons being substituted for the pure and intelligible Idea of God? This is precisely what was feared by the Iconoclasts, whose millennial quarrel is still with us today. Their rage to destroy images arose precisely because they sensed this omnipotence of simulacra, this facility they have of effacing God from the consciousness of men, and the overwhelming, destructive truth which they suggest: that ultimately there never has been any God, that only the simulacrum exists, indeed that God himself has only ever been his own simulacrum. Had they been able to believe that images only masked the Platonic Idea of God, there would have been no reason to destroy them. One can live with the idea of a distorted truth. But their metaphysical despair came from the idea that in fact they were not images . . . but actually perfect simulacra forever radiant with their own fascination.[15]

Baudrillard obviously intends to suggest that the postmodern era presents us with a similar crisis of faith. Not only is there no referent, no absolute or individual subject, but the complete triumph of commodity culture means that the concepts, such as labour-power and use-value, which were created as tools to critique the commodity, are also obsolete and 'ideological'. However, this need not necessarily mean that there is no longer any way of distinguishing truth from falsehood. It means, rather, that true consciousness can no longer be distinguished from false by virtue of its closer accordance with some external reality. In *For a Critique of the Political Economy of the Sign*, Baudrillard designated the consumer mentality a 'slave morality' (62). In *The Mirror of Production*, as in Foucault, it is clear that the subject is enslaving itself: 'the master–slave couple is interiorized in the same individual without ceasing to function as an alienated structure' (104). Here, perhaps, we can discern a ray of hope. Even though the consumer society reduces its subjects to objects, there remains, apparently, some residual resource within the individual which might enable us to struggle against the all-pervasive power of commodification. In his later work, Baudrillard chooses not to follow this course, and instead glories in the disarray of the transcendental subject. The implications of his earlier analyses have, however, been explored by others, most notably by the Slovene philosopher, Slavoj Zizek.

LIVING A LIE: ZIZEK AND PRACTICAL FETISHISM

It seems clear that, in the postmodern world, it is no longer useful to divide our experience into the 'levels' of ideas, matter and representation. This means that any notion of ideology in the sense of a differentiated sphere of ideas must be abandoned. As Ernesto Laclau and Chantal Mouffe note in *Hegemony and Socialist Strategy* (1985), 'the very notion of representation as transparency becomes untenable. What is actually called into question here, is the base/superstructure model itself.'[16] Representation no longer mediates between an ideal and a material sphere, it does not refer to any other level of experience. Furthermore, Laclau and Mouffe use

Foucault's concept of 'discourse' to denote material practice as well as systems of representation, thereby assuming that there is no significant distinction between these spheres. As with Foucault's 'fascism in the head', this means that the struggle against oppression must take place at all levels, since 'a fragmentation of positions exists *within* the social agents themselves' (84). In the postmodern world the personal is the political, and the individual subject, rather than the broader canvas of world history, is the proper focus of political practice.

The question which postmodern theory often neglects is *why* the material/ideal/representation model has collapsed. There is general agreement that the category of representation is fundamental; there is nothing outside representation. For the early Baudrillard, this triumph of representation is a kind of perversion, which is directly traceable to 'the virtual international autonomy of finance capital . . . the uncontrollable play of floating capital'.[17] Money is calcified representation, and it is 'the total artificiality of the sign that one "adores" in money'.[18] It is the money-form, the principle of abstract equivalence, which exemplifies objectified representation. The unprecedented dominance of finance capital thus extends representation into material practice, and also into the minds of human subjects.

This effect of commodity fetishism on the individual psyche is Zizek's primary concern. Due to the fact that he views this effect as malign and distorting, Zizek revives the concept of ideology in order to describe it. He does not, however, return to the notion that ideology consists purely of ideas. Like Debord, he assumes that real life has itself become ideological. Ideology is not false because it does not correspond to material reality; it does this all too well. The problem is with material reality itself, which has taken the grotesque shape of an objectified illusion, and this illusion is duplicated in our consciousness. As Zizek notes in *Tarrying with the Negative* (1993), ideology can only be understood as a phenomenon involving the Hegelian totality:

> For Hegel, the inverted 'topsy-turvy world' does not consist in presupposing, beyond the actual, empirical world, the kingdom of suprasensible ideas, but in a kind of double inversion by means of which these suprasensible ideas themselves assume again sensible form, so that the very sensible world is re-doubled . . . he does *not* put forward another, even 'deeper' supra-Ground which would ground the ground itself; he simply grounds the ground in the totality of its relations to the grounded content.[19]

So 'ideology' is not something which affects only our ideas, it is something which happens to the totality of our existence, including material practice. It is not to be conceived as a misapprehension of reality, but as a distortion in the form taken by reality itself. As Zizek puts it in *The Sublime Object of Ideology* (1989):

> ideology is not simply a 'false consciousness', an illusory representation of reality, it is rather this reality itself which is already to be conceived as 'ideological' – *'ideological' is a social reality whose very existence implies the non-knowledge of its participants as to its essence*. . . . 'Ideological' is not the *'false consciousness' of a social being but this being in so far as it is supported by 'false consciousness'.*[20]

We must differentiate here between Zizek's notion of 'false consciousness' and the concept of illusion. There is nothing illusory about ideology, which accurately corresponds to reality. In that reality, however, we systematically behave as if an illusion were true. The illusion referred to is the autonomy of representation, as expressed in the market economy. We know that money is only a representation of a determinate amount of human activity, but we nevertheless base our whole economy, and thus the material activity of our everyday lives, on the assumption that money is a thing-in-itself – an assumption which we know to be false. In Zizek's words:

When individuals use money, they know very well that there is nothing magical about it – that money, in its materiality, is simply an expression of social relations. The everyday spontaneous ideology reduces money to a simple sign giving the individual possessing it a right to a certain part of the social product. So, on an everyday level, the individuals know very well that there are relations between people behind the relations between things. The problem is that in their social activity itself, in what they are *doing*, they are *acting* as if money, in its material reality, is the embodiment of wealth as such. They are fetishists in practice, not in theory.[21]

The autonomy of representation is thus objectively true, but ontologically false, and ethically reprehensible. Zizek has no quarrel with the postmodern declarations that metaphors of depth are untenable, that we can never 'get beyond' signification, or that the subject is an effect of representation. But he points out that this situation is paralleled in the finance-based economy, and he indicates that the effects of this economy on the individual subject are dire indeed. In fact, Zizek goes so far as to say that the commodity economy destroys the subject. This is the point at which Zizek's divergence from the neo-Foucauldians is most pronounced. Foucault, as we have seen, also announces the death of the subject. But he does not connect this event to commodification, and he therefore sees it as an entirely positive development. This position is enthusiastically endorsed by postmodern theory as a whole. In *Tarrying with the Negative*, Zizek raises his standard against this kind of theory:

Far from containing any kind of subversive potentials, the dispersed, plural, constructed subject hailed by postmodern theory (the subject prone to particular, inconsistent modes of enjoyment, etc.) simply designates *the form of subjectivity that corresponds to late capitalism*. Perhaps the time has come to resuscitate the Marxist insight that Capital is the ultimate

> power of 'deterritorialization' which undermines every fixed
> social identity, and to conceive of 'late capitalism' as the epoch
> in which the traditional fixity of ideological positions (patriar-
> chal authority, fixed sexual roles, etc.) becomes an obstacle to
> the unbridled commodification of everyday life.
>
> (216)

Once we admit that such postmodern phenomena as the objectified subject, the autonomy of representation, the impossibility
of teleology, and the disappearance of the referent are effects of
commodity fetishism, then postmodern ideology begins to look
decidedly unappetizing. When we recall that commodity fetishism
involves the triumph of dead labour over living labour, the postmodern world begins to seem positively sinister. If we remember
the metaphysical horror with which previous eras confronted
the fetishism of objects, as well as the moralistic dismay with
which they viewed usury and finance, we must conclude that they
would have seen the triumph of abstract representation which
characterizes postmodernism as the victory of pure evil. Why does
it not seem that way to us?

THE LATE ADORNO

Zizek, then, agrees with Foucauldian postmodernism that ideology
is material practice. This contention can be traced to Althusser's
slide from the legitimate claim that ideas must be *expressed in*
material form before they can be known, to the illegitimate and
contradictory assertion that ideas *are* material – an assumption
which then informs Foucault's influential account of 'discourse'.
However, there are two vital differences between Zizek's view
of this situation and the way it is portrayed by conventional postmodernism. First, Zizek sees the materialization of ideology as an
unmitigated catastrophe. It means, he thinks, that we are literally
living a lie. Because we live it, however, the lie becomes real.
The postmodern condition is thus one in which reality itself

s false; and not merely false but dehumanizing, destructive, and
evil in the profoundest sense of the word. Second, Zizek arrives
at the view that ideology is material through a dialectical analysis
of the totality. He does not collapse the ideal into the material,
in an Althusserian reduction. Instead, he describes a process
of fetishism which operates on the material, representational
and ideal levels simultaneously, without any one of these levels
determining' this process. This is necessarily so, because he defines
fetishization as a perversion of the relationships between these
levels. The material world is organized in a manner which presupposes that the ideal and the representational are themselves
material. Logically, of course, the ideal and the representational
are not material. But the dreadful prospect which Zizek confronts
is that this mode of practical organization turns out to be
self-fulfilling: it reduces the ideal and the representational to the
material in practice. And this can and does occur despite the
fact that the ideal and the representational are demonstrably not
material in theory.

If it is to remain true to itself, then, theory must be rigorously
and consistently opposed to the real, to the factual. The most
promising attempt to elaborate such a theory is undertaken by
Theodor Adorno, in his late masterpiece *Negative Dialectics*
(1966). As he puts it in his introduction, 'dialectics is the ontology
of the wrong state of things' (11); it is the study of the real as the
false. The central image which haunts this book was coined by
Max Weber, at the end of *The Protestant Ethic*. Weber remarks that
in the seventeenth century, when capitalist forms of economic
practice were just beginning, it was assumed that

> the care for external goods should only lie on the shoulders of
> the 'saint like a light cloak, which can be thrown aside at any
> moment.' But fate decreed that the cloak should become an
> iron cage.
>
> (Weber, 181)

As the figure implies, commodity fetishism has become all encompassing. The formal structure of the commodity determine our hopes and dreams, our philosophical systems, our mode of signification, our economic practice. It hardly matters which 'level', if any, determines the others – the problem is one of form and it affects all levels simultaneously and to the same degree. A Adorno puts it:

> Where ideology is no longer added to things as a vindication o complement – where it turns into the seeming inevitability and thus legitimacy of whatever is – a critique that operates with the unequivocal causal relation of superstructure and infrastructure is wide of the mark.
>
> (268

Negative Dialectics is an attempt, if not to unlock Weber's cage then at least to make us aware of its existence. In the introduction Adorno makes it clear he does not accept the notion – which we saw espoused by Baudrillard – that use-value is merely an ideolog ical effect produced by exchange-value. The cage, that is to say is not empty; there is something real imprisoned within it. In the Marxist conception, exchange-value is the principle of false identity. It renders different use-values identical for the purposes of exchange. Baudrillard would say that these use-values are illusions produced retrospectively in the act of exchange. Adorno recoils in horror from such an idea, going so far as to declare that 'the in effable part of the utopia is that which defies subsumption under identity – the "use-value" in Marxist terminology – is necessary anyway if life is to go on at all' (11). Of course, it is by no mean necessary that life *should* go on at all. In fact, Adorno is decidedly pessimistic about the long-term prospects for life, and his pessimism is deduced from the undeniable prevalence and power of exchange-value. Because of his belief that use-value is truer than exchange-value, however, Adorno does not see the current dominance of the market as inevitable. In a passage which criticizes the postmodernism of Foucault or Lyotard *avant la lettre*, he points out that

> Determinism acts as if dehumanization, the totally unfolded merchandise character of the working capacity, were human nature pure and simple. No thought is given to the fact that there is a limit to the merchandise character: the working capacity that has not just an exchange-value but a use-value. To deny free will outright means to reduce men unreservedly to the normal merchandise form of their labor in full-fledged capitalism.
>
> (264)

However, Adorno would certainly agree that, under capitalism, people really have become objectified. His aim is to register this fact, while simultaneously showing that it is wrong, and that it could have been and might still be otherwise. This is the paradox of ideology: 'Barter as a process has real objectivity and is objectively untrue at the same time. . . . This is why, of necessity, it will create a false consciousness: the idols of the market' (190). Among these Baconian 'idols' is the subject itself:

> The universal domination of mankind by the exchange-value – a domination which a priori keeps the subjects from being subjects and degrades subjectivity itself to a mere object – makes an untruth of the general principle that claims to establish the subject's predominance. The surplus of the transcendental subject is the deficit of the utterly reduced empirical subject.
>
> (178)

It is important to do justice to the full complexity of Adorno's thought here. He claims that human beings are originally both subject and object. Under capitalism, however, they are made into mere objects. Their subjectivity is, as it were, squeezed out of them, and it reconstitutes itself in the fantasy form of a transcendental subject. In our society, this transcendental subject is 'man': a supposedly eternal and irreducible apotheosis of human nature. As though to compensate for their loss of real subjectivity, each of the individual 'subjects' (who are in fact no longer subjects but objects) then acquires an illusory, ideological 'appearance' of subjectivity, which is based on an identification with the fantastic transcendental subject. On an individual level, we end up with fully objectified subjects who take their very objectivity as a form of subjectivity. For example, a postmodern individual may well construct his or her 'personality' out of an amalgam of consumer goods, fashion statements, 'lifestyle' choices, identification with real or fictional celebrities – in other words, out of objective phenomena which are administered to them by the 'culture industry'. And yet this utter loss of subjectivity is combined, in our society, with a resounding emphasis on the 'individual', on the uniqueness of each and every 'person'. As Adorno shrewdly sees, this is a shabby ideological ruse: 'to a great extent the subject came to be an ideology, a screen for society's objective functional context and a palliative for the subject's suffering under society' (66–7).

There are thus two subjects: a 'real' subject, which is repressed by exchange-value, and an 'objective' subject, which is not 'real', and which is the product of exchange-value. This might not even matter, except for the fact that the relationship between these two subjects is antagonistic: we are faced with 'the subject as the subject's foe' (10). The 'objective' subject is like a zombie in a horror movie, preying upon and destroying the 'real' subject. We can find an early parable of this development in Mary Shelley's *Frankenstein* (1818). When Dr Frankenstein is confronted by the monster he has created, the creature reminds him that 'thou hast made me more powerful then thyself',[22] and suggests that the only way the doctor can be rid of him is literally to close his eyes to the monster's presence. The doctor cries

'Begone! relieve me from the sight of your detested form.'
'Thus I relieve thee, my creator,' he said and placed his hated
hands before my eyes, which I flung from me with violence;
'thus I take from thee a sight which you abhor.'

(210)

.idley Scott's movie *Blade Runner* suggests an intensification of
his process, in which the sinister Tyrrel Corporation has succeeded
n creating 'replicants' of human beings who are unaware of their
wn artificial status. The ubiquitous theme of death-in-life, of the
ving dead, in recent popular culture is highly revealing, and
ighly disturbing. In *Nineteen Eighty-Four* (1949), George Orwell
onnects the motif of the unsuspecting zombie to totalitarian
olitics. The book's hero, Winston Smith, cannot understand his
ver's optimism:

'We are the dead,' he said. 'We're not dead yet,' said Julia
prosaically. 'Not physically. . . . But it makes very little difference.
So long as human beings stay human, death and life are the
same thing.'[23]

n *Negative Dialectics*, Adorno takes Marx's description of capitalism
s the domination of dead labour over living labour to its terrible
onclusion. The consequences of this position are so frightening
1at it is easy to understand why many thinkers – Althusser and
oucault among them – recoil from them, and take refuge in the
otion that the subject was actually an object all along. Adorno
onsiders this option, and pointedly rejects it:

But it is not the purpose of critical thought to place the object
on the orphaned royal throne once occupied by the subject. On
that throne the object would be nothing but an idol. The
purpose of critical thought is to abolish the hierarchy.

(181)

/e must remember, however, that postmodern capitalism has
ready abolished the hierarchy of subject and object. It has done

so, according to Adorno, in a radically false way: by collapsing th
opposition into one of its poles, and reducing the subject to a
object. It is this illegitimate reduction which constitutes the forr
presently taken by 'ideology':

> With society, ideology has so advanced that it no longer evolve
> into a socially required semblance and thus to an independer
> form, however brittle. All that it turns into is a kind of glue: th
> false identity of subject and object.
>
> (34?

It follows that a theory which is critical of ideology must resist th
temptation to endorse such an identity:

> The task of criticizing ideology is to judge the subjective ar
> objective shares and their dynamics. It is to deny the false obje
> tivity of concept fetishism by reducing it to the social subject, ar
> to deny false subjectivity, the sometimes unrecognizably veile
> claim that all being lies in the mind, by showing it up as a frauc
> a parasitical nonentity, as well as demonstrating its immaner
> hostility to the mind.
>
> (197–?

Once again, we find 'the subject as the subject's foe'. Adorn
obviously perceives the postmodern subject as animated by som
mysterious drive to self-destruction. In a highly significar
recourse to metaphysical terminology, he refers to this tendency a
a 'spell', under which 'Men become that which negates then
(344).

What is this force which 'negates' human beings? Adorno tell
us that the 'spell' is 'radical evil' (346); that 'In human experienc
the spell is the equivalent of the fetish character of merchandis
(ibid.); and that 'In the spell, the reified consciousness has becom
total' (ibid.). This 'spell', then, clearly involves objectification – i
is objectification as applied to human beings. The name which w
usually give to this thing is 'death'. Death is the ultimate false (bu

eal) objectification. The fetishism of the commodity, no less than
he idolatry of the heathen, brings death in its wake:

> As subjects live less, death grows more precipitous, more
> terrifying. The fact that it literally turns them into things makes
> them aware of reification, their permanent death and the form
> of their relations that is partly their fault. The integration of
> death in civilization, a process without power over death and a
> ridiculous cosmetic procedure in the face of death, is the shap-
> ing of a reaction to this social phenomenon, a clumsy attempt
> of the barter society to stop up the last holes left open by the
> world of merchandise.
>
> (370)

To fetishize a commodity or to worship an idol is to treat dead
abour, dead life, as though it were alive. It is to misconstrue
he relationship between death and life. If this were merely an
deological error, it might not be very important. But, in front of
Adorno's stricken gaze, this ideology reveals its practical results.
First of all, the instrumental reason to which the commodity form
gives birth shows every sign of culminating in nuclear annihilation,
or by rendering the earth ecologically uninhabitable. This is what
happens when we fetishize our own reason, making of it a 'second
nature' (67). At least these catastrophes have not yet actually
happened. However, Adorno believes that we have already
witnessed the consequences of objectifying human activity, in the
Nazi Holocaust:

> The earthquake of Lisbon sufficed to cure Voltaire of the
> theodicy of Leibniz, and the visible disaster of the first nature
> was insignificant in comparison with the second, social
> one, which defies human imagination as it distills a real hell
> from human evil . . . since, in a world whose law is universal
> individual profit, the individual has nothing but this self that
> has become indifferent, the performance of the old, familiar

tendency is at the same time the most dreadful of things. There
is no getting out of this, no more than out of the electrified
barbed wire around the camps. Perennial suffering has as
much right to expression as a tortured man has to scream;
hence it may have been wrong to say that after Auschwitz
you could no longer write poems. But it is not wrong to raise
the cultural question whether after Auschwitz you can go on
living – especially whether one who escaped by accident, one
who by rights should have been killed, may go on living.
His mere survival calls for the coldness, the basic principle of
bourgeois subjectivity, without which there could have been
no Auschwitz; this is the drastic guilt of him who was spared.
By way of atonement he will be plagued by dreams such as that
he is no longer living at all, that he was sent to the ovens in
1944 and his whole existence since has been imaginary,
an emanation of the insane wish of a man killed twenty years
earlier.

(361–3)

The one who 'was spared' referred to in this passage is, of course,
Adorno himself. In a notion which gives a disturbing twist to the
'death of the author', he speculates that the words he is writing
may be nothing more than the dreams of a dead man. And there
is a sense in which his philosophy bears this out. The ultimate
message of *Negative Dialectics* is that 'we are the dead': our
economic system presupposes it, our consciousness reflects it, our
material activity puts it into practice. The iron cage, Adorno
concludes, is constructed on death row.

CONCLUSION

On 13 February 1995, an internal memo was issued to the 'Emerging Markets Group' of a major US bank. It reported on the financial consequences of a peasant revolt in southern Mexico and it read, in part:

> While Chiapas, in our opinion, does not pose a fundamental threat to Mexican political stability, it is perceived to be so by many in the investment community. The government will need to eliminate the Zapatistas to demonstrate their effective control of the national territory and of security policy.

Thus does objectified human activity, or capital, enter into a hostile and contradictory relationship with actual human subjects. The Mexican government is urged to crush the uprising not because it poses a threat, but because of a perception that it poses a threat. This perception is attributed to 'the investment community'. Who makes up 'the investment community'? Can this 'community' be identified with a group of individual human beings? Or is 'the investment community' merely a euphemistic personification of the impersonal, abstract and inhuman power of international capital?

In *Capital* Marx writes that in a money economy 'the character who appear on the economic stage are merely personification of economic relations' (179). For a while, the forces of 'capital' and 'labour' appeared to be embodied in certain social classes. This i not necesarily the case, however. The germinal form of the capital labour opposition can be traced to Hegel's dialectic of master and slave in the *Phenomenology* (111–9). Hegel demonstrates that thi polarity is mutually defining, so that the seemingly 'independent identity of the master actually depends upon the objectified identity of the slave. In Marx, the apparently independent operations of capital are unmasked as the spectral reflections of objectified human labour. The former are incarnated in a parasitic class of 'capitalists and the latter in a class of 'proletarians' who sell themselves for wages. By this definition, however, everyone in Western society is now a proletarian. Furthermore, many of these proletarians also own capital – 'the investment community' includes pension funds and personal bank accounts as well as stocks and shares. Who then, are the postmodern capitalists? Is it possible that today, a Baudrillard claims, 'the master–slave couple is interiorized in the same individual'?[1]

The history of capitalism involves the progressive domination of exchange over production, a process which instigates the hege-mony of representation over reality and collapses the subject into an object. Today, the production of things is far less profitable than the exchange of the representations of things – bigger fortunes are made by transferring figures across computer screens than by building factories. The West has turned into a consumer society and this means that mass consumption must be induced in the population. This is done through the stimulation of desires by advertising and marketing, and also through the extension of large-scale consumer credit. The word 'credit' means 'to believe', and small-scale credit rests on the belief of the creditor in the 'character of the debtor. As Marx noted, this is already an abstraction from the real character of an individual. But today, credit has become completely divorced from character. When the first federal insurance funds were set up to guarantee bank deposits, protests were raised on precisely these grounds: one US senator complained the idea would obviate the need for trust, and so 'make the individual a nonentity'.[2]

If money is a representation of subjective activity, then credit – a promise to pay money – is an abstraction from a representation. By the 1980s, the world economy had long functioned through credit rather than through money. During that decade, credit became so ubiquitous and (thanks to federal insurance) so free of risk, that the mere expectation of receiving credit, or 'credit-worthiness' was sufficient to enable one to purchase entire corporations. In the paradigmatic instances of junk bonds and Third World debt, the ability to repay the debt, and so the question of 'character', became effectively irrelevant to the capacity to obtain credit.

We can thus see how subjective factors such as 'character', 'confidence' and 'trust' are progressively removed from their original applications to actual human beings. These subjective qualities are abstracted and alienated, and they thereby achieve a determining power over the affairs of real human subjects. It is in the service of the 'confidence' of 'the investment community' that the Mexican government sends its troops into Chiapas. On what does this 'confidence' depend? On a perception. A perception is a subjective phenomenon. But the subject which experiences this perception is a wholly objectified subject: 'the investment community' is actually nothing more than a set of figures on an electronic screen. The 'investment community' is, in fact, pure representation. It represents subjective activity, subjective decisions, subjective experiences like 'trust' and 'confidence', in objective form. The autonomy of representation turns the subject into an object. It is thus the apotheosis of ideology. But ideology can only occur *within* a subject: it is only the subject which objectifies its self. Could the subject not also, in principle, reverse this process? And if so, how?

NOTES

INTRODUCTION

1   Martin Amis: *Money*; Penguin Books; London, 1984, 31.
2   The most convincing answers to this question are given by Frederic Jameson in *Postmodernism, or, the Cultural Logic of Late Capitalism*; Duke University Press; Durham, 1991. The following account draws its inspiration from Jameson's description of postmodernism.
3   Richard Rorty: 'Postmodernist Bourgeois Liberalism', in *Postmodernism: A Reader*, ed. Thomas Docherty; Columbia University Press; New York, 1993, 325.
4   The constitutive role of language, and of signification in general, which characterizes postmodern philosophy, was first outlined by Ferdinand de Saussure, in *Course on General Linguistics*, trans. Roy Harris; Open Court; La Salle, Illinois, 1986.
5   Thus Jean-François Lyotard declares 'the answer is this: war on totality'. *The Postmodern Explained: Correspondence 1982–1985*, ed. Julian Pefanis and Morgan Thomas, trans. Don Barry, Bernadette Maher, Julian Pefanis, Virginia Spate and Morgan Thomas; University of Minnesota Press; Minneapolis, 1993, 16.
6   Andrew Ross (ed.): *Universal Abandon? The Politics of Postmodernism*; University of Minnesota Press; Minneapolis, 1988, xiv–xv.
7   Paul A. Bové: 'The Ineluctability of Difference: Scientific Pluralism and the Critical Intelligence', in Jonathan Arac (ed.): *Postmodernism and Politics*; University of Minnesota Press; Minneapolis, 1986, 17.
8   All examples are from. Julian Lewis Watkins: *The 100 Greatest Advertisements: Who Wrote Them and What They Did*; Dover Publications; New York, 1959, 37, 34, 40.
9   William Leach: *Land of Desire: Merchants, Power, and the Rise of a New American Culture*; Pantheon Books; New York, 1993, 385.
10 Max Weber: *The Protestant Ethic and the Spirit of Capitalism*, trans. Talcott Parsons; Unwin Hyman; London, 1930, 56. Subsequent references are to this edition.

1 ORIGINS

1   Plato: *The Republic*, trans. G.M.A. Grube; Hackett Publishing Co.; Indianapolis, 1974, 515b–516a.
2   Aristotle: *Politics*, trans. Carnes Lord; University of Chicago Press;

Chicago, 1984, 1254al, 36–42, 40. Subsequent references are to this edition.

3 Aristotle: *Magna Moralia*, book I, 1186al, 4–17, in *The Complete Works of Aristotle*, vol.II (the Revised Oxford Translation), ed. Jonathan Barnes; Princeton University Press; Princeton, 1984, 187. Subsequent references are to this edition.

4 *Nicomachean Ethics*, book II, 1103b, 2–6.

5 From 'The Church Militant' (*c.* 1633), ll.111–20, in *The English Poems of George Herbert*, ed. C.A. Patrides; J.M. Dent & Sons; London, 1986.

6 Fulke Greville: 'A Treatise of Monarchy', in *The Remains*, ed. G.A. Wilkes; Oxford University Press; Oxford, 1965. Subsequent references are to this edition.

7 See, for example, J.G.A. Pocock: *The Machiavellian Moment: Florentine Political Thought and the Atlantic Republican Tradition*; Princeton University Press; Princeton, 1975. See also Hans Baron: *The Crisis of the Early Italian Renaissance: Civic Humanism and Republican Liberty in an Age of Classicism and Tyranny*; Princeton University Press; Princeton, 1966.

8 Girolamo Savonarola: 'Treatise on the Constitution and Government of the City of Florence', in *Humanism and Liberty: Writings on Freedom from Fifteenth-century Florence*, trans. and ed. Renee Nea Watkins; University of South Carolina Press; Columbia, S.C., 1978, 237.

9 Niccolò Machiavelli: *The Prince*, in *Works*, vol.II, trans. Anthony J. Pancini; Greenvale Press; Greenvale, N.Y., 1969, 247. Subsequent references are to this edition.

10 Martin Luther: *Works*, vol.I, ed. Jaroslav Pelikan and Helmut T. Lehmann; Fortress Press; Philadelphia, 1959, 28. Subsequent references are to this edition.

11 The modern edition cited is John Bunyan: *The Pilgrim's Progress*; Oxford University Press, Oxford, 1984, 19–20.

12 Francis Bacon: *Novum Organon*, trans. R. Ellis and James Spedding; George Routledge & Sons Ltd.; London, 1959, 70. Subsequent references are to this edition.

EMPIRICISM

1 John Milton: *Eikonoklastes* (1649), in *Complete Prose Works*, vol.III; Yale University Press; New Haven, 1962, 601. Subsequent references are to this edition.

2   John Milton: *Complete English Poems*, vol.XII, ed. Gordon Campbell Everyman; Lymington, Hants., 1990, 90–5.

3   Milton, *The Judgement of Martin Bucer Concerning Divorce* (1644) vol.II, 439.

4   Psalm 115, 1.4.

5   Cited by Lowell W. Coolidge in Milton's *Complete Prose Works*, vol.II 222 n.1.

6   Milton had married, and shortly afterwards been deserted by, a young woman whom he found personally and politically uncongenial.

7   Thomas Hobbes, *Leviathan*, ed. C.B. MacPherson; Penguin Books London, 1985, 85–6. Subsequent references are to this edition.

8   Note that this development entails a shift from ontology to epistemology.

9   Milton, *Of Education*, in *Complete Prose Works*, vol.II, 366–7.

10 Cited in Graham Greene: *Lord Rochester's Monkey*; Penguin Books London, 1974, 165.

11 This point is made by C.B. MacPherson, in *The Political Theory of Possessive Individualism, Hobbes to Locke*; Oxford University Press Oxford, 1969.

12 John Locke: *An Essay Concerning Human Understanding*; William Tegg London, 1867, 59. Subsequent references are to this edition.

13 Condillac: *Essay on the Origin of Knowledge*, in *Eighteenth-Century Philosophy*, ed. Lewis White Beck; Free Press; New York, 1966, 170.

14 Helvetius: *Essays on the Mind* (1758); Burt Franklin; New York, 1970 177.

15 Holbach: *The System of Nature*, trans. H.D. Robinson; Burt Franklin New York, 1970, 11. Subsequent references are to this edition.

16 Friedrich Nietzsche: *Human, All-Too-Human*, part two, trans. Paul V. Cohn, in *The Complete Works*, vol.VII; T.N. Foulis; London, 1911, 184

17 Jean-Jacques Rousseau: *Discourse on the Origin of Inequality*, trans. Donald A. Cress; Hackett Publishing Co.; Indianapolis, 1992, 13 Subsequent references are to this edition.

18 William Wordsworth: *Selected Prose*, ed. John O. Hayden; Penguin Books; London, 1988, 282.

19 John Keats: *The Letters of John Keats 1795–1821*, vol.I, ed. Hyder Edward Rollins; Harvard University Press; Cambridge, Mass., 1958, 185.

20 See Simon Schama: *Citizens*; Alfred A. Knopf; New York, 1989, 778–9 and 834–41.

21 Cited in Schama, 574.

22 Edmund Burke: *Reflections on the Revolution in France*, ed. William B

Todd; Holt, Rinehart & Winston; New York, 1965, 211. Subsequent references are to this edition.

23   All quotations from Shakespeare are taken from *The Riverside Shakespeare*, ed. G. Blakemore Evans; Houghton Mifflin Co.; Boston, 1974.

24   Cited in Emmet Kennedy: *Destutt de Tracy and the Origins of 'Ideology'*; American Philosophical Society; Philadelphia, 1978, 19.

25   'Réponse à l'adresse du Conseil d'Etat' 20 December 1812; cited in Kennedy, 215.

26   Ibid., 45.

27   Ibid., 189.

28   Ibid., 145.

29   Hans Barth: *Truth and Ideology*, trans. Frederic Lilge; University of California Press; Berkeley, 1976, 4. In this respect, Destutt's 'ideology' anticipates twentieth-century structuralism, which also claims to explain the genesis of other modes of thought by reference to a linguistic model.

30   Maine de Biran, quoted in Kennedy, 100.

3 IDEALISM

1   Johann Wolfgang von Goethe: *Faust*, trans. Peter Salin; Bantam Books; New York, 1985.

2   Johann Wolfgang von Goethe: *The Sufferings of Young Werther*, trans. Bayard Quincy Morgan; Frederick Ungar Publishing Co.; New York, 1957, 21.

3   In *The Philosophical Works of Descartes*, vol.I, trans. Elizabeth S. Haldane and G.R.T. Ross; Cambridge University Press; Cambridge, 1911, 10. Subsequent references are to this edition.

4   *Discourse on the Method*, 101.

5   Quoted in Bertrand Russell: *A History of Western Philosophy*; Simon & Schuster; New York, 1945, 648.

6   As Christopher Norris notes in *What's Wrong with Postmodernism*; Johns Hopkins University Press; Baltimore, 1990.

7   Immanuel Kant: *Critique of Pure Reason*, trans. J.M.D. Meiklejohn; J.M. Dent & Sons; London, 1934, 1.

8   S.T. Coleridge: *Biographia Literaria*, vol.I, ed. J. Shawcross; Oxford University Press; Oxford, 1969, 202.

9   William Wordsworth: *Poems*, ed. Stephen Gill; Oxford University Press; Oxford, 1984, 298.

10   Samuel Taylor Coleridge: *Complete Poetical Works*, ed. Ernest Hartley
      Coleridge; Clarendon Press; Oxford, 1912, 365.
11   Immanuel Kant: *Critique of Judgment*, trans. Werner S. Pluhar; Hackett
      Publishing Co.; Indianapolis, 1987, 14–15. Subsequent references are
      to this edition.
12   The noun 'Vorstellung' is traditionally translated as 'representation'.
      Pluhar declines this option on the grounds that it falsely implies
      that Kant's theory of perception is representational. See 14 n.17.
13   For an incisive critique of the postmodern reading of Kant, see
      Christopher Norris: *The Truth about Postmodernism*; Blackwell; Oxford,
      1993.
14   G.W.F. Hegel: *Phenomenology of Spirit*, trans. A.V. Miller; Clarendon
      Press; Oxford, 1977, 2. Subsequent references are to this edition.
15   W.B. Yeats: *The Poems*, ed. Richard J. Finneran; Macmillan; New York,
      1989, 259.
16   David Strauss: *The Life of Jesus*, trans. George Eliot, in *The Young
      Hegelians*, ed. Lawrence S. Stepelevich; Cambridge University Press;
      Cambridge, 1983, 25. Subequent references are to this edition.
17   *The Young Hegelians*, 211, 227.
18   H. Glockner, cited in Sidney Hook: *From Hegel to Marx*; University of
      Michigan Press; Ann Arbor, 1962, 220 n.1.
19   Ludwig Feuerbach: *The Essence of Christianity*, trans. George Eliot;
      Harper & Brothers Publishers; New York, 1957, xxxiii. Subsequent ref-
      erences are to this edition.

4 MARXISM

1   Thomas Carlyle: *Sartor Resartus* (1830), cited in *The Norton Anthology
     of English Literature*, vol.II; Norton; New York, 1993, 935.
2   Karl Marx: *The German Ideology*, in Karl Marx and Friedrich Engels:
     Collected Works, vol.V; International Publishers; New York, 1975, 36–7.
     Unless otherwise specified, subsequent references to Marx and
     Engels are to this edition.
3   Baron Alfred Tennyson: *The Poems*, ed. Christopher Ricks; Longmans;
     Harlow, 1969, 697.
4   The account of *The Eighteenth Brumaire* in this chapter builds upon
     readings given in Jeffrey Mehlman: *Revolution and Repetition*;
     University of California Press; Berkeley, 1979; Terry Eagleton: *Walter
     Benjamin, or, Towards a Revolutionary Criticism*; Verso; London, 1981;
     and Christopher Norris: *The Truth about Postmodernism*; Blackwell;
     Oxford, 1993.

5   Marx uses the English word, to indicate a generic term for the petty bourgeoisie.

6   See Karl Marx: *Capital*, vol.I, trans. Ben Fowkes; Penguin Books; London, 1976, 125–77. Subsequent references to *Capital* are to this edition.

7   Thomas Traherne: *Centuries*; Morehouse Publishing; Wilton, CT, 1985, 114–15.

8   Cited in this form by Marx in the *Economic and Philosophical Manuscripts* (III, 323–4), and in abbreviated form in *The German Ideology* (V, 230–1) as well as in *Capital*, 229 n.42.

9   Jean-Paul Sartre: *Nausea*, trans. Lloyd Alexander; New Directions Publishing Co.; New York, 1957, 10.

10 Georg Simmel: *The Philosophy of Money*, trans. Tom Bottomore and David Frisby from a first draft by Kaethe Mengelberg; Routledge; London, 1978, 68. Subsequent references are to this edition.

11 Friedrich Engels, in *The Correspondence of Karl Marx and Frederick Engels*; International Publishers; New York, 1942, 475–6.

12 George Plekhanov: *The Materialist Conception of History*; International Publishers; New York, 1940, 19. Subsequent references are to this edition.

13 V.I. Lenin: *Materialism and Empirio-Criticism*; International Publishers; New York, 1927, 125–6.

14 Georg Lukács: *History and Class-consciousness*, trans. Rodney Livingstone; MIT Press; Cambridge, Mass., 1971, 170. Subsequent references are to this edition.

15 Marx: Preface to *A Contribution to the Critique of Political Economy*, cited in Antonio Gramsci: *Selections from the Prison Notebooks*, ed. and trans. Quintin Hoare and Geoffrey Nowell-Smith; International Publishers; New York, 1971, 365 n.54. Subsequent references to Gramsci are to this edition.

POST-MARXISM

1   Cited by Walter Benjamin in *Aesthetics and Politics*, ed. Ronald Taylor, trans. Harry John; New Left Books; London, 1977, 97.

2   Louis Althusser: 'Ideology and Ideological State Apparatuses', in *Lenin and Philosophy and Other Essays*, trans. Ben Brewster; Monthly Review Press; New York, 1971, 145. Subsequent references are to this edition.

3   Louis Althusser: *For Marx*, trans. Ben Brewster; Pantheon Books; New York, 1969, 34. Subsequent references are to this edition.

4   Cited in *The Norton Anthology of English Literature*, vol.I, 519.

5   Pierre Macherey: *A Theory of Literary Production*, trans. Geoffrey Wall; Routledge; London, 1978, 44. Subsequent references are to this edition.

6   Pierre Macherey and Etienne Balibar: 'On Literature as an Ideological Form: Some Marxist Propositions', *Praxis* 5 (1981), 43–58, 46. Subsequent references are to this edition.

7   T.S. Eliot: *Collected Poems*; Harcourt, Brace & World; New York, 1970, 83.

8   Ernst Bloch: 'Discussing Expressionism' (1938), trans. Rodney Livingstone, in *Aesthetics and Politics*, ed. Ronald Taylor; New Left Books; London, 1977, 22.

9   Georg Lukács: 'Realism in the Balance' (1938), trans. Rodney Livingstone, in *Aesthetics and Politics*, 34.

10   Theodor Adorno: 'Reconciliation under Duress' (1961), trans. Rodney Livingstone, in *Aesthetics and Politics*, 160.

11   Theodor Adorno: 'Letter to Walter Benjamin' (1935), trans. Harry Zohn, in *Aesthetics and Politics*, 111.

12   Max Horkheimer: 'On the Problem of Truth', in *The Essential Frankfurt School Reader*, ed. Andrew Arato and Eike Gebhardt; Urizen Books; New York, 1978, 433. Subsequent references are to this edition.

13   Max Horkheimer: 'The End of Reason', in *The Essential Frankfurt School Reader*, 31.

14   Theodor W. Adorno: 'On the Fetish Character in Music and the Regression of Listening', in *The Essential Frankfurt School Reader*, 290.

15   Theodor W. Adorno and Max Horkheimer: *Dialectic of Enlightenment*, trans. John Cumming; Herder & Herder; New York, 1972, 126. Subsequent references are to this edition.

16   *The Essential Frankfurt School Reader*, 45.

17   *Dialectic of Enlightenment*, xv.

18   Herbert Marcuse: *One-dimensional Man: Studies in the Ideology of Advanced Industrial Society*; Beacon Press; Boston, 1964, 12.

19   Max Weber: *The Protestant Ethic and the Spirit of Capitalism*, trans. Talcott Parsons; Unwin Hyman; London, 1930, 17. Subsequent references are to this edition.

20   Sigmund Freud: *Three Essays on the Theory of Sexuality*, trans. James Strachey; Basic Books Inc.; New York, 1962, 19.

21   Sigmund Freud: *Totem and Taboo: Some Points of Agreement between the Mental Lives of Savages and Neurotics*, trans. James Strachey; W.W. Norton; London, 1950, 32. Subsequent references are to this edition.

22 *Dialectic of Enlightenment*, 6.

23 *Dialectic of Enlightenment*, 28.

24 Ngugi Wa Thiong'O: *Devil on the Cross*; Heinemann International; Oxford, 1982, 172–3.

25 Ferdinand de Saussure: *Course in General Linguistics*, trans. Roy Harris; Open Court; La Salle, 1972, 6. Subsequent references are to this edition.

26 Claude Lévi-Strauss: *The Savage Mind*; University of Chicago Press; Chicago, 1966, 15. Subsequent references are to this edition.

27 Michael Taussig: *The Devil and Commodity Fetishism in South America*; University of North Carolina Press; Chapel Hill, 1980, 36, 181.

28 V.N. Volosinov: *Marxism and the Philosophy of Language*, trans. Ladislav Matejka and I.R. Titunik; Harvard University Press; Cambridge, Mass., 1973, cited in the translators' preface, 2. Subsequent references are to this edition.

29 Roland Barthes: *Mythologies*, trans. Annette Lavers; Hill & Wang; New York, 1994, 116.

6 POSTMODERNISM

1 Theodor Adorno: *Negative Dialectics*, trans. E.B. Ashton; Routledge; London, 1990, 267–8. Subsequent references to Adorno are to this edition.

2 Jean Baudrillard: *Symbolic Exchange and Death*, trans. Iain Hamilton Grant; Sage Publications; London, 1993, 2.

3 Friedrich Nietzsche: *On the Genealogy of Morals*, trans. Walter Kaufmann and R.J. Hollingdale; Vintage Books; New York, 1969, 27–8. Subsequent references are to this edition.

4 Michel Foucault: *The Order of Things: An Archaeology of the Human Sciences*, trans. Alan Sheridan-Smith; Pantheon Books; New York, 1970, ix. Subsequent references are to this edition.

5 Michel Foucault: *The Archaeology of Knowledge*, trans. A.M. Sheridan Smith; Pantheon Books; New York, 1972, 12. Subsequent references are to this edition.

6 Michel Foucault: *The History of Sexuality*, trans. Robert Hurley; Vintage Books; New York, 1990, 93.

7 As anyone who has suffered through the opening pages of *Discipline and Punish* can testify.

8 Michel Foucault: *Power/Knowledge: Selected Interviews and Other Writings 1972–1977*, ed. Colin Gordon, trans. Colin Gordon, Leo

Marshall, John Mepham and Kate Soper; Pantheon Books; New York, 1980, 58. Subsequent references are to this edition.

9   Michel Foucault: *Remarks on Marx: Conversations with Duccio Trombadori*, trans. R. James Goldstein and James Cascaito; Semiotext (e); New York, 1991, 120.

10 Michel Foucault: *Politics, Philosophy, Culture: Interviews and Other Writings 1974–1984*, ed. Lawrence D. Kritzman, trans. Alan Sheridan et al.; Routledge; New York, 1988, 26.

11 See *Politics, Philosophy, Culture*, 26

12 Guy Debord: *Society of the Spectacle*; Black & Red; Detroit, 1967, no. 217. Debord scorns such bourgeois pretensions as publisher's rights; subsequent references are nevertheless to this edition.

13 Jean Baudrillard: *For a Critique of the Political Economy of the Sign*, trans. Charles Levin; Telos Press; St Louis, 1981, 146. Subsequent references are to this edition.

14 Jean Baudrillard: *The Mirror of Production*, trans. Mark Poster; Telos Press; St Louis, 1975, 122. Subsequent references are to this edition.

15 Jean Baudrillard: *Simulations*, trans. Paul Foss, Paul Patton and Philip Beitchman; Semiotext (e); New York, 1983, 8–9.

16 Ernesto Laclau and Chantal Mouffe: *Hegemony and Socialist Strategy: Towards a Radical Democratic Politics*; Verso; London, 1985, 58. Subsequent references are to this edition.

17 *The Mirror of Production*, 129 n.9.

18 *For a Critique of the Political Economy of the Sign*, 93.

19 Slavoj Zizek: *Tarrying with the Negative: Kant, Hegel, and the Critique of Ideology*; Duke University Press; Durham, 1993, 138–9. Subsequent references are to this edition.

20 Slavoj Zizek: *The Sublime Object of Ideology*; Verso; New York, 1989, 21.

21 *The Sublime Object of Ideology*, 31.

22 Mary Shelley: *Frankenstein, or the Modern Prometheus*; G. & W.B. Whittaker; London, 1823, 206. Subsequent references are to this edition.

23 George Orwell: *Nineteen Eighty-Four*; Harcourt, Brace & Co.; New York, 1949, 137.

CONCLUSION

1   *The Mirror of Production*, 104.

2   Cited in James Grant: *Money of the Mind*; Farrar Straus Giroux; New York, 1992, 138. Grant's ideas inform the paragraph that follows.

FURTHER READING

The following is a selection of other secondary and introductory volumes which consider many of the same issues as this book.

Barth, Hans (1976) *Truth and Ideology*, trans. Frederic Lilge; University of California Press; Berkeley. [An original and opinionated over-view, relating Marxist thought to the nihilistic tradition of Nietzsche.]

Eagleton, Terry (1990) *The Ideology of the Aesthetic*; Basil Blackwell Ltd.; Oxford. [Deals with the relations between ideology, pleasure and idealist philosophy.]

—— (1991) *Ideology: an Introduction*; Verso; London. [The definitive introduction to the subject. Takes a Marxist, historical approach, and simultaneously puts forward the author's own thesis.]

—— (1994) *Ideology*; Longman Group UK; Harlow, Essex. [A selection of readings by authors ranging from Marx to Clifford Geertz. Offers a wide variety of definitions.]

Ingersoll, David E. and Matthews, Richard K. (1986) *The Philosophic Roots of Modern Ideology: Liberalism, Communism, Fascism*; Prentice-Hall Inc.; Englewood Cliffs, N.J.. [Traces the evolution of various forms of ideology, as well as considering the phenomenon as a whole.]

Larrain, Jorge (1979) *The Concept of Ideology*; Hutchinson & Co.; London. [Penetrating and undogmatic historical account of ideology's various permutations.]

Mannheim, Karl (1936) *Ideology and Utopia*, trans. Louis Wirth and Edward Shils; Harcourt, Brace & Co.; New York. [Brilliant early attempt to theorize ideology across various periods. Defines it against the rival force of 'utopia'.]

McLellan, David (1986) *Ideology*; University of Minnesota Press; Minneapolis. [Brief, schematic but extremely lucid outline of the topic, which addresses the issue of its continuing relevance.]

Thompson, John B. (1990) *Ideology and Modern Culture: Critical Social Theory in the Age of Mass Communication*; Stanford University Press Stanford. [Masterly analysis of the role of the mass media in th definition and transmission of idelogy.]

BIBLIOGRAPHY

Adorno, Theodor (1990) *Negative Dialectics*, trans. E.B. Ashton; Routledge; London.

Adorno, Theodor and Horkheimer, Max (1972) *Dialectic of Enlightenment*, trans. John Cumming; Herder & Herder; New York.

Althusser, Louis (1969) *For Marx*, trans. Ben Brewster; Pantheon Books; New York.

—— (1971) *Lenin and Philosophy and Other Essays*, trans. Ben Brewster; Monthly Review Press; New York.

Amis, Martin (1984) *Money*; Penguin Books; London.

Appleby, Joyce Oldham (1978) *Economic Thought and Ideology in Seventeenth-century England*; Princeton University Press; Princeton.

Arac, Jonathan (ed.) (1986) *Postmodernism and Politics*; University of Minnesota Press; Minnesota.

Arato, Andrew and Gebhardt, Eike (eds) (1978) *The Essential Frankfurt School Reader*; Urizen Books; New York.

Aristotle (1984) *Complete Works*, ed. Jonathan Barnes; Princeton University Press; Princeton.

—— (1984) *Politics*, trans. Carnes Lord; University of Chicago Press; Chicago.

Bacon, Francis (1959) *Novum Organon*, trans. R. Ellis and James Spedding; George Routledge & Sons Ltd; London.

Baron, Hans (1966) *The Crisis of the Early Italian Renaissance*; Princeton University Press; Princeton.

Barthes, Roland (1994) *Mythologies*, trans. Annette Lavers; Hill & Wang; New York.

Baudrillard, Jean (1975) *The Mirror of Production*, trans. Mark Poster; Telos Press; St Louis.

—— (1981) *For a Critique of the Political Economy of the Sign*, trans. Charles Levin; Telos Press; St Louis.

—— (1983) *Simulations*, trans. Paul Foss, Paul Patton and Philip Beitchman; Semiotext (e); New York.

—— (1993) *Symbolic Exchange and Death*, trans. Iain Hamilton Grant; Sage Publications; London.

Beck, Lewis White (ed.) (1966) *Eighteenth-century Philosophy*; Free Press; New York.

Bunyan, John (1984) *The Pilgrim's Progress*; Oxford University Press; Oxford.

Burke, Edmund (1965) *Reflections on the Revolution in France*, ed. William B. Todd; Holt, Rinehart & Winston; New York.

Carlyle, Thomas (1956) *Sartor Resartus: on Heros and Hero-worship*; Dutton; New York.

Coleridge, S.T. (1912) *Complete Poetical Works*, ed. Ernest Hartley Coleridge; Clarendon Press; Oxford.

—— (1969) *Biographia Literaria*, ed. J. Shawcross; Oxford University Press; Oxford.

Debord, Guy (1967) *Society of the Spectacle*; Black & Red; Detroit.

Descartes, René (1911) *Philosophical Works*, trans. Elizabeth S. Haldane and G.R.T. Ross; Cambridge University Press; Cambridge.

Destutt de Tracy (1826–7) *Elemens d'Ideologie*; A. Wahlen; Brussels.

Docherty, Thomas (ed.) *Postmodernism: A Reader*; Columbia University Press; New York.

Eagleton, Terry (1981) *Walter Benjamin, or, Towards a Revolutionary Criticism*; Verso; London.

Eliot, T.S. (1970) *Collected Poems*; Harcourt, Brace & World; New York.

Feuerbach, Ludwig (1957) *The Essence of Christianity*, trans. George Eliot; Harper & Brothers Publishers; New York.

Fitzgerald, F. Scott (1991) *The Great Gatsby*; Cambridge University Press; New York.

Foucault, Michel (1970) *The Order of Things: An Archaeology of the Human Sciences*, trans. Alan Sheridan-Smith; Pantheon Books; New York.

—— (1972) *The Archaeology of Knowledge*, trans. A.M. Sheridan Smith; Pantheon Books; New York.

—— (1977) *Discipline and Punish: the Birth of the Prison*, trans. Alan Sheridan; Pantheon Books; New York.

—— (1980) *Power/Knowledge: Selected Interviews and other Writings 1972–7*, ed. Colin Gordon, trans. Colin Gordon, Leo Marshall, John Mepham and Kate Soper; Pantheon Books; New York.

—— (1988) *Politics, Philosophy, Culture: Interviews and Other Writings, 1974–84*, ed. Lawrence D. Kritzman, trans. Alan Sheridan *et al.*; Routledge; New York.

—— (1990) *The History of Sexuality*, vol.I, trans. Robert Hurley; Vintage Books; New York.

—— (1991) *Remarks on Marx: Conversations with Duccio Trombadori*, trans. R. Jame Goldstein and James Cascaito; Semiotext (e); New York.

Freud, Sigmund (1962) *Three Essays on the Theory of Sexuality*, trans. James Strachey; Basic Books Inc.; New York.

—— (1950) *Totem and Taboo: Some Points of Agreement between the Mental Lives of Savages and Neurotics*, trans. James Strachey; W.W. Norton; London.

Goethe, Johann Wolfgang von (1957) *The Sufferings of Young Werther*, trans. Bayard Quincy Morgan; Frederick Ungar Publishing Co.; New York.

—— (1962) *Faust*, trans. Peter Salm; Bantam Books; New York.

Goux, Jean-Joseph (1990) *Symbolic Economies*, trans. Jennifer Curtiss Gage; Cornell University Press; Ithaca.

Gramsci, Antonio (1971) *Selections from the Prison Notebooks*, ed. and trans. Quintin Hoare and Geoffrey Nowell-Smith; International Publishers; New York.

Grant, James (1992) *Money of the Mind*; Farrar Strauss Giroux; New York.

Greene, Graham (1974) *Lord Rochester's Monkey*; Penguin Books; London.

Greville, Fulke (1965) *The Remains*, ed. G.A. Wilkes; Oxford University Press; Oxford.

Hegel, G.W.F. (1977) *Phenomenology of Spirit*, trans. A.V. Miller; Clarendon Press; Oxford.

Helvetius, Claude (1970) *Essays on the Mind*; Burt Franklin; New York.

Herbert, George (1986) *The English Poems*, ed. C.A. Patrides; J.M. Dent & Sons; London.

Hobbes, Thomas (1985) *Leviathan*, ed. C.B. MacPherson; Penguin Books; London.

Holbach, Baron d' (1970) *The System of Nature*, trans. H.D. Robinson; Burt Franklin; New York.

Hook, Sidney (1962) *From Hegel to Marx*; University of Michigan Press; Ann Arbor.

Jameson, Frederic (1991) *Postmodernism, or, the Cultural Logic of Late Capitalism*; Duke University Press; Durham.

Kant, Immanuel (1934) *Critique of Pure Reason*, trans. J.M.D. Meikelejohn; J.M. Dent & Sons; London.

—— (1987) *Critique of Judgment*, trans. Werner S. Pluhar; Hackett Publishing Co.; Indianapolis.

Keats, John (1958) *The Letters*, ed. Hyder Edward Rollins; Harvard University Press; Cambridge, Mass.

Kennedy, Emmet (1978) *Destutt de Tracy and the Origins of 'Ideology'*; American Philosophical Society; Philadelphia.

Laclau, Ernesto and Mouffe, Chantal (1985) *Hegemony and Socialist Strategy: Towards a Radical Democratic Politics*; Verso; London.

Leach, William (1993) *Land of Desire: Merchants, Power and the Rise of a New American Culture*; Pantheon Books; New York.

Lenin, V.I. (1927) *Materialism and Empirio-Criticism*; International Publishers; New York.

Lévi-Strauss, Claude (1966) *The Savage Mind*; University of Chicago Press; Chicago.

Locke, John (1867) *An Essay Concerning Human Understanding*; William Tegg; London.

Lukács, Georg (1971) *History and Class-consciousness*, trans. Rodney Livingstone; M.I.T. Press; Cambridge, Mass.

Luther, Martin (1959) *Works*, ed. Jaroslav Pelikan and Helmut T. Lehmann; Fortress Press; Philadelphia.

Lyotard, Jean-François (1984) *The Postmodern Condition: A Report on Knowledge*, trans. Geoff Bennington and Brian Massumi; University of Minnesota Press; Minneapolis.

—— (1993) *Libidinal Economy*, trans. Iain Hamilton Grant; Indiana University Press; Bloomington.

—— (1993) *The Postmodern Explained: Correspondence 1982–1985*, ed. Julian Pefanis and Morgan Thomas, trans. Don Barry, Bernadette Maher, Julian Pefanis, Virginia Spate and Morgan Thomas; University of Minnesota Press; Minneapolis.

Macherey, Pierre (1978) *A Theory of Literary Production*, trans. Geoffrey Wall; Routledge; London.

Machiavelli, Niccolò (1969) *Works*, trans. Anthony J. Pancini; Greenvale Press; Greenvale, N.Y.

MacPherson, C.B. (1969) *The Political Theory of Possessive Individualism, Hobbes to Locke*; Oxford University Press; Oxford.

Marcuse, Herbert (1964) *One-dimensional Man: Studies in the Ideology of Advanced Industrial Society*; Beacon Press; Boston.

Marx, Karl (1976) *Capital*, vol.I, trans. Ben Fowkes; Penguin Books; London.

Marx, Karl and Engels, Friedrich (1975) *Collected Works*; International Publishers; New York.

Mehlman, Jeffrey (1979) *Revolution and Repetition*; University of California Press; Berkeley.

Milton, John (1962) *Complete Prose Works*; Yale University Press; New Haven.

—— (1990) *Complete English Poems*; ed. Gordon Campbell; Everyman; Lymington, Hants.

Ngugi Wa Thiong'O (1982) *Devil on the Cross*; Heinemann International; Oxford.

Nietzsche, Friedrich (1911) *Complete Works*, trans. Paul V. Cohn; T.N. Fouls; London.

—— (1969) *On the Geneology of Morals*, trans. Walter Kaufman and R.J. Hollingdale; Vintage Books; New York.

Norris, Christopher (1990) *What's Wrong with Postmodernism*; Johns Hopkins University Press; Baltimore.

—— (1993) *The Truth About Postmodernism*; Blackwell; Oxford.

Orwell, George (1949) *Nineteen Eighty-Four*; Harcourt, Brace & Co.; New York.

lato (1974) *The Republic*, trans. G.M.A. Grube; Hackett Publishing Co.; Indianapolis.

ekhanov, George (1940) *The Materialist Conception of History*; International Publishers; New York.

ocock, J.G.A. (1975) *The Machiavellian Moment: Florentine Political Thought and the Atlantic Republican Tradition*; Princeton University Press; Princeton.

oss, Andrew (ed.) (1988) *Universal Abandon? The Politics of Postmodernism*; University of Minnesota Press; Minneapolis.

ousseau, Jean-Jacques (1992) *Discourse on the Origin of Inequality*, trans. Donald R. Cress; Hackett Publishing Co.; Indianapolis.

ussell, Bertrand (1945) *A History of Western Philosophy*; Simon & Schuster; New York.

aussure, Ferdinand de (1972) *Course in General Linguistics*, trans. Roy Harris; Open Court; La Salle.

artre, Jean-Paul (1957) *Nausea*, trans. Lloyd Alexander; New Directions Publishing Co.; New York.

chama, Simon (1989) *Citizens*; Alfred E. Knopf; New York.

hakespeare, William (1974) *The Riverside Shakespeare*, ed. G. Blakemore Evans; Houghton Mifflin Co.; Boston.

helley, Mary (1823) *Frankenstein, or the Modern Prometheus*; G. & W.B. Whittaker; London.

immel, George (1978) *The Philosophy of Money*, trans. Tom Bottomore, David Frisby and Kaethe Mengelberg; Routledge; London.

tepelevich, Lawrence S. (1983) *The Young Hegelians*; Cambridge University Press; Cambridge.

aussig, Michael (1980) *The Devil and Commodity Fetishism*; University of North Carolina Press; Chapel Hill.

Taylor, Charles (1975) *Hegel*; Cambridge University Press; Cambridge.

Taylor, Ronald (ed.) (1977) *Aesthetics and Politics*; New Left Books; London.

Tennyson, Alfred, Baron (1969) *The Poems*, ed. Christopher Ricks; Longmans; Harlow, Essex.

Traherne, Thomas (1985) *Centuries*; Morehouse Publishing; Wilton, CT.

Volosinov, V.N. (1973) *Marxism and the Philosophy of Language*, trans. Ladislav Matejka and I.R. Titunik; Harvard University Press; Cambridge, Mass.

Watkins, Julian Lewis (1959) *The 100 Greatest Advertisements*; Dover Publishers; New York.

Watkins, Renee Nea (ed.) (1978) *Humanism and Liberty: Writings on Freedom from Fourteenth-century Florence*; University of South Carolina Press; Columbia, S.C.

Weber, Max (1930) *The Protestant Ethic and the Spirit of Capitalism*, trans. Talcott Parsons; Unwin Hyman; London.

Wordsworth, William (1984) *Poems*, ed. Stephen Gill; Oxford University Press; Oxford.

—— (1988) *Selected Prose*, ed. John O. Hayden; Penguin Books; London.

Yeats, W.B. (1989) *The Poems*, ed. Richard J. Finneran; Macmillan; New York.

Zizek, Slovoj (1989) *The Sublime Object of Ideology*; Verso; New York.

—— (1993) *Tarrying with the Negative: Kant, Hegel, and the Critique of Ideology*; Duke University Press; Durham.